M O U N T   V E R N O N

THE
CIVIL
WAR
YEARS

it . . . . might, at lea

. . sacred remains

. . hope is disappointe

. . to the immortal . .

. . occasion by hands

. . tion . of the United

. . are prepared to .

. . ungainly indebted, fo

MOUNT VERNON

THE CIVIL WAR YEARS

PREVIOUSLY PUBLISHED AS

PRESENCE OF A LADY

BY DOROTHY TROTH MUIR

WITH A NEW INTRODUCTION BY ERNEST B. FURGURSON
FOREWORDS BY ROBERT E. LEE IV
AND ULYSSES GRANT DIETZ

MOUNT VERNON LADIES' ASSOCIATION
MOUNT VERNON, VIRGINIA
1993

LIBRARY OF CONGRESS CATALOGING-IN-PUBLICATION DATA
MUIR, DOROTHY TROTH, 1905-1988.
MOUNT VERNON : THE CIVIL WAR YEARS / WITH A NEW INTRODUCTION BY ERNEST B.
FURGURSON; FOREWORDS BY ROBERT E. LEE IV AND ULYSSES GRANT DIETZ. — REV. ED.
P. CM.
REV. ED. OF: PRESENCE OF A LADY / BY DOROTHY TROTH MUIR. 1946.
INCLUDES INDEX.
ISBN 0-931917-26-3 (SOFTCOVER) : $10.95
1. MOUNT VERNON (VA. : ESTATE) — HISTORY — 19TH CENTURY. I. MUIR, DOROTHY TROTH,
1905-1988. PRESENCE OF A LADY. II. MOUNT VERNON LADIES' ASSOCIATION OF THE UNION.
III. TITLE.
E312.5.M88 1993
93-34872
973.7'1 — DC20
CIP

BOOK DESIGN BY

GLENN A. HENNESSEY

WASHINGTON, DC

In Grateful Appreciation

The publication of *Mount Vernon: The Civil War Years*, which includes the formerly published *Presence of a Lady*, has been made possible through the generous contributions of family members of Mrs. Lucien M. Hanks, Regent of the Mount Vernon Ladies' Association from 1943 to 1948 and Vice Regent for Wisconsin from 1914 through 1956. The Mount Vernon Ladies' Association expresses its special thanks to:

Mr. and Mrs. William Vilas Hanks

Mr. and Mrs. John Doyle Short

Master Bradley Ryan Short

Miss Julia Haley Short

Mr. and Mrs. William Vilas Hanks III

Miss Katherine Ryan Hanks

Master William Patrick Hanks

Mrs. Louise H. Davis

Mrs. Lucien Hanks, Jr.

Mr. and Mrs. Richard E. Adams, Jr.

Mr. James J. Hanks, Jr.

Dr. and Mrs. John B. Hanks

Mrs. James Judge Hanks

Miss Molly Hanks

Acknowledgment

The author wishes to express her grateful thanks to the Mount Vernon Ladies' Association of the Union for graciously granting her permission to read and copy Miss Tracy's letters, which have been carefully preserved in the Archives at Mount Vernon.

She wishes to thank, also, Mr. Charles C. Wall, Superintendent of the Mount Vernon Ladies' Association, and Miss Irene Warren, the Librarian, for the help they gave her each time she visited Mount Vernon, for the purpose of research; and Mr. Orin West Winn, Mr. Kirk C. Wilkinson, and the late Mr. Charles H. Callahan, for the help they gave her during the writing of *Presence of a Lady*.

Dorothy Troth Muir

1946

Dedication

To Mrs. Lucien M. Hanks, Regent
Mount Vernon Ladies' Association of the Union

Contents

ULYSSES GRANT DIETZ

Mount Vernon is a peculiarly powerful symbol. Although far more modest physically than most of the celebrated buildings in and around Washington, D.C., it is the most emotionally powerful place to me in the entire area. Unlike the various landmark memorials and government buildings – and even the White House, which is more a governmental icon than a house – Mount Vernon has always been first and foremost a home. In visiting Mount Vernon earlier this year with friends from Washington who had never been there, I was immediately struck by two things: the sense of realness about the plantation, which is fairly astounding given its long history as a very popular tourist attraction; and secondly, the shock of seeing how small this house really is, despite its grandiose pretensions.

Compared to the English houses it was meant to emulate, Mount Vernon is hardly more than a comfortable villa. Yet it was, in America, representative of the American dream, even as that dream was being formulated in the early years of the republic.

George Washington was clearly riding a wave of popularity when he triumphantly returned to Mount Vernon in 1783 following the Revolutionary War. But Washington did not view Mount Vernon as the throne from which he would rule over an American kingdom. He recognized the inherent dangers of drifting toward monarchy, and he avoided any chance of the United States ever becoming the sort of kingdom from which it had just freed itself. The idea of a royal nation must have been tempting, and it was perhaps Washington's most heroic act that he refused to take the bait. The very modesty of Mount Vernon compared with the great English country houses of the time is epitomatic of how America was – and is – different from its mother country. Mount Vernon, for all its pretensions, was a middle–class vision, a vision of comfort and plenty.

There is another irony that Mount Vernon represents to us. As the home of America's liberator and first president, it was also the corporate headquarters of a great southern planter and slave owner. Mount Vernon is symbolic both of what made this country strong at its birth and of the inner weaknesses that almost tore it apart in the middle decades of the 19th century. And, of course, that's where my family comes into the picture.

One of the great mysteries to me is that there is no evidence that Ulysses S. Grant and his wife, Julia, ever visit-ed Mount Vernon. In *Presence of a Lady*, a visit from Mary Lincoln, wife of Abraham Lincoln, is carefully recorded. I cannot believe that neither General Grant, an ardent life-long admirer of George Washington, nor his wife, who grew up in a slave-owning plantation in St. Louis, did not visit Mount Vernon repeatedly during their many years in Washington. There is no question, however, that the Grants and their descendants often called Washington their home. I can only assume that Mount Vernon was as much a symbolic part of their lives as it has been in mine.

Mount Vernon must have been a very poignant place for Julia Grant. The Civil War tore her own family apart, pitting cousins against cousins and families against families. Undoubtedly, she would have seen Mount Vernon as the ultimate romanticization of everything she felt about her own family plantation, White Haven, where she spent a pampered and idyllic childhood surrounded by a retinue of slave girls.[1] The jarring of the American ideal of equality and the realities of the southern slave economy were probably never resolved in her mind. Mount Vernon would have been every bit as evocative a place to Julia as it would have to have been to Mrs. Robert E. Lee, and not for dissimilar reasons. Julia first came to know Washington in the middle of the war, when Ulysses was made commander of all the Union armies. She records in her diary her first visit to the city, as well as meeting with the Lincolns at the White House.[2] She also recalls a boat trip from Washington to Richmond, just after the South's capital fell to the Union forces. Looking out at the riverbank, listening to the

1   GRANT, JULIA DENT. THE PERSONAL MEMOIRS OF JULIA DENT GRANT (MRS. ULYSSES S. GRANT). NEW YORK: G. P. PUTNAM'S SONS, 1975, P. 36.
2   IBID, P. 129.

frogs chirping,

I fell to thinking of all the sad tragedies of the past four years. How many homes made desolate! How many hearts broken! How much youth sacrificed! How much treasure lost! And tears, great tears, fell from my eyes. For what, I could not tell. Could it be that my visit reminded me of my dear old home in Missouri?[3]

For Ulysses S. Grant, however, Mount Vernon would have had a different, though related, sort of symbolism. To him it would have symbolized the ideal that anyone in America could be president, that anyone could make it to the top. He was from far more average stock than his wife. Descended from Puritans and Scottish immigrants, he was born into the world of small shopkeepers and artisans. His entry into West Point and his subsequent military career (with all its ups and downs) was his ticket to the American dream. His own attempts at farming in Missouri, despite his wife's affluent family, were rather dismal. His log house, Hardscrabble, was a far cry from the high portico and sweeping lawns at Mount Vernon, or even from his father-in-law's piazza at White Haven. The Grants had slaves, too, some of whom were given to the young couple as a wedding present by Julia's parents in 1848. One of the greatest ironies of Grant's life is that his nemesis, Robert E. Lee, freed his slaves at Arlington *before* Grant freed his.

But the most powerful symbolism that Mount Vernon would have held for Ulysses S. Grant was as a symbol of the

3 IBID, PP. 150-151.

Union. If Grant had one ultimate goal throughout the brutal and cruel years of the war, it was the preservation of the Union. For those who have never experienced a civil war first hand, it is hard to imagine the fear of losing that union, that special sense of "nation." Without question, the Grants must have been conscious of Mount Vernon throughout the war, standing alone, isolated in its own little neutral world, as the madness of the war raged around it. While I have no claim to any expertise on the Civil War, I know that while Ulysses S. Grant may have enjoyed the strategizing and the planning, he was always struck by the devastation and waste of the Civil War. Perhaps it was the symbol of Mount Vernon, of George Washington's American dream, that kept him going to the bitter end.

Once the war was over, especially as Grant's political career began to pick up momentum, the city of Washington would be forever intertwined with the family's life. Despite the fact that the only surviving Grant house is in Galena, Illinois (excepting the house where Grant died in Mt. McGregor, New York, which did not belong to the Grants), and the fact that they were very much a part of New York society for years after the presidency, Washington became "home" to the Grants.

The connection with the capital city began in 1865, shortly after Lincoln's assassination. Having settled into an elegant house in Philadelphia, Julia found herself more and more alone with the children, due to Ulysses's increasing time in Washington. Eventually he persuaded her to give up that house and move south. By the beginning of 1866, they were comfortably settled in a large house in Georgetown Heights, purchased with a 10-year mortgage for $30,000.[4] From this point on, regardless of where they lived or traveled, it was to Washington that they would return.

In the early 1880s, before the failure of the former president's law firm, Grant & Ward, which would cloud the last years of Ulysses's life, the Grants visited Washington to seek comfort in old friendships and familiar surroundings. Julia expressed this sentiment in her characteristic way in her memoirs:

Dear Washington, how I love you, with your beautiful, broad, generous streets and blue skies! The sun shines always there for me.

Grant's financial collapse, coming just before the onset of the throat cancer that would ultimately kill him, prevented them from spending much time in Washington during their final years together. Julia stayed in New York only a few years following the death of Ulysses, in spite of the financial security created by the publication of her husband's cele-brated memoirs. She eventually moved back to her beloved Washington in 1894 and remained there until her own death in 1902.[5]

Like his father, Frederick Dent Grant pursued a military career and spent most of his adult life between New York and Washington. Although his military work kept him on the road for most of his life, Fred's wife, Ida, moved back to

4 IBID, PP. 160-161.
5 IBID, P. 23.

Washington after his death in 1912. She lived in a house on New Hampshire Avenue, maintaining one of the last of the horse-drawn carriages in the city, until her death in 1930.

Both of Fred and Ida's children also spent most of their lives tied to Washington. Their daughter Julia was born in the Lincoln Bedroom in the White House in her grandfather's last year in office, 1876. She eventually married, of all things, a Russian prince, and spent 20 years in Russia. But, after the 1917 revolution, Princess Cantacuzene, Countess Speransky, born Julia Grant, came back to Washington and lived out the remainder of her 99 years in the city of her birth.

Fred and Ida's son Ulysses S. Grant III, my grandfather, followed his father and grandfather through West Point and into an army career, also becoming a general. He, too, moved around a good deal in the course of his career. Most of his life, however, was focused on Washington, which was always home to him and his children.

One aspect of Ulysses S. Grant III's career not only ties him closely to Washington and Mount Vernon, but to my own life. What really brought Grandfather to Washington was his role in the Army Corps of Engineers and his passion for city planning and historic preservation. In the 1930s, he was the Executive and Disbursing Officer of the National Capital Park and Planning Commission. He was in charge of the maintenance and preservation of Pierre Charles L'Enfant's original plan for the capital city, and it was one of the central interests of his professional life. He supervised the design and construction of the Mount Vernon Memorial Parkway that connected the capital with the first president's plantation.[6] To him it was imperative that the nation's capital be physically – and thus psychologically – connected with the place of its spiritual birth, Mount Vernon. My grandfather was also president of the Washington National Monument Association, and he helped oversee the ongoing care and preservation of the Washington Monument.

In 1948, he was one of the founders of what would later be called the National Trust for Historic Preservation, head-quartered in Washington and dedicated to the preservation of this country's architectural and historic treasures.[7] He was also intimately involved with the ongoing restoration and preservation of the historic fabric of the White House itself and served as one of its early curators.[8]

Of special interest to me is one of my grandfather's last major preservation efforts. As a private citizen in Washington, he became President of the Columbia (now Washington) Historical Society. At a moment of crisis in this Society's history, my grandfather found a new home for the Society, and at the same time preserved an important Washington landmark through the acquisition of the Christian Heurich Mansion on New Hampshire Avenue in 1955.[9]

---

6 "THE PLAN OF WASHINGTON, ADDRESSES BY CHARLES W. ELIOT II AND COL. ULYSSES S. GRANT III," IN THE SIXTY-THIRD ANNUAL REPORT OF THE FAIRMOUNT PARK ART ASSOCIATION. PHILADELPHIA: BY THE ASSOCIATION, 1935.

7 HE WAS PRESIDENT OF THE NATIONAL COUNCIL FOR HISTORIC SITES AND BUILDINGS IN 1947. HE WROTE THE INTRODUCTORY ESSAY IN THE NATIONAL TRUST'S FIRST PUBLICATION ENTITLED PRESERVING AMERICA'S HERITAGE (WASHINGTON, 1947).

8 SEE WILLIAM SEALE'S NEW BOOK, THE WHITE HOUSE (NEW YORK, 1992), FOR DETAILS OF HIS WORK IN THIS PROJECT.

9 SEE MEREDITH B. COLKET, JR., "GENERAL GRANT AND THE CHRISTIAN HEURICH MEMORIAL MANSION," IN RECORDS OF THE COLUMBIA HISTORICAL SOCIETY. WASHINGTON, D.C.: BY THE SOCIETY, 1968.

On the surface it may appear that the Heurich Mansion –
an ornate Victorian beer-baron's home – is a far cry from
George Washington's pastoral, neoclassical plantation on the
banks of the Potomac River. I confess that the reason I find it
so significant a chapter in the Grant family history is really
in its ties to my own life and career. For Ulysses S. Grant's
grandson, the Heurich Mansion probably symbolized something quite different, and yet not unrelated to Mount
Vernon's symbolism. Just as Mount Vernon stands as a
reminder of this country's beginnings in the 18th-century
agrarian ideal, so the Heurich Mansion stands for the
America of the industrial 19th century, where European
immigrants, such as Christian Heurich, could achieve the
American dream in the heart of George Washington's ideal
capital. Ulysses S. Grant had risen to achieve the American
dream in Washington, and my grandfather must have seen a
subtle but meaningful similarity in this wealthy brewer's
house. Sadly, Victorian buildings were being bulldozed right
and left in 1955, and the Heurich Mansion is a rare survivor
in Washington. I am particularly touched by my grandfather's foresight because I was born in 1955. When my
grandfather died, I had never learned a great deal about his
professional career nor his life in Washington. Yet, I must
have inherited something from him other than his name. As
Curator of Decorative Arts at the Newark Museum in New
Jersey, I am an avid historic preservationist, and one of my
responsibilities is the John Ballantine House, another

Mount Vernon, painted by William Trost Richards in 1855, depicting the mansion
as it appeared shortly before the beginning of the Civil War and three years before the Mount Vernon
Ladies' Association purchased the estate.

Collection of The Newark Museum. Gift of Mr. and Mrs. Snowden Henry, 1966.

Victorian mansion once owned by a wealthy beer brewer.[10]
My deep respect for this landmark helps me to understand
what my grandfather saw in his adopted city of Washington,

10   AS AN ASIDE, BOTH GRANT'S HARDSCRABBLE FARM AND THE DENT FAMILY'S PLANTATION
     WHITE HAVEN ARE NOW OWNED AND PRESERVED BY YET ANOTHER BEER BREWER,
     ANHEUSER-BUSCH. ANHEUSER-BUSCH IS TODAY THE ONLY REMAINING BEER BREWER IN
     NEWARK, NEW JERSEY.

and I can only imagine that my great–great–grandfather viewed Mount Vernon with a certain degree of awe and untold respect.

In the collection of the Newark Museum is a painting of the Mount Vernon mansion at sunset, painted in 1855 by William Trost Richards. It is a rare and important picture, one of the few paintings done of Mount Vernon at this period, just before its nick–of–time salvation by the Mount Vernon Ladies' Association. The house is bathed in a rosy glow – the setting sun of a bygone era – while a new moon appears over the Potomac in the east. Perhaps the moon symbolizes hope for the future of the house. In any case, neither the artist nor the Mount Vernon Ladies' Association quite foresaw the gathering storm, or the bleak years of hardship during the war. But this painting reminds us all that Mount Vernon was then, and remains today, a symbol of this country's enduring ideals that touches everyone who knows its remarkable story.

ROBERT E. LEE IV

George Washington and Robert E. Lee each played an integral part in weaving the fabric of education in America. Despite the numerous, uncanny parallels that can be drawn to connect these two men, their respective contributions to the developing educational system in America remain one of their most lasting accomplishments. Washington and Lee were confronted with the need to quickly establish a solid educational foundation in this country following difficult wars on American soil.

On the surface, this interest of Washington's, expressed time after time, is surprising. The son of a Virginia planter, Washington never received any formal education. His step–brothers, Lawrence and Augustine, had been sent to study in England as was proper for young men of his family's stature. Unfortunately, their father's untimely death closed the door on George's opportunity to be educated abroad. Throughout his life, Washington regretted this setback. A lack of formal education, however, did not prevent him from becoming its patron in later life, nor did it slow the progress of his remarkable career.

George Washington was self–educated. He successfully acquainted himself with the diverse subjects treated in the nearly 900 books he collected for his library. Much of what he learned through books he put into practice developing Mount Vernon into an 18th–century plantation. Acting as father and grandfather to his wife Martha's children from a previous marriage, he was determined to provide them with a sound education through reputable schools and good tutors. Too often Washington's influence did little to move his adopted family, as in the cases of his stepson, John Parke Custis, and his stepgrandson, George Washington Parke Custis.

The most compelling evidence that attests to George Washington's interest in education is his will. Washington summed up his entire life's concern for education in this remarkable document. A just and equitable man, Washington provided for the freedom of his slaves, effective after the death of his wife. After that time, however, he required that the slaves be brought up in some useful occu–pation and taught to read and write.

Also in his will, Washington gave $4,000 to the Alexandria Academy in order to establish a "free" school to educate orphan children, as well as the children of poor or indigent parents. Washington further freed two of his nephews from their indebtedness to him for paying nearly $5,000 to advance their education, including room and board.

The most interesting comment that Washington made

on the subject of education pertains to his indefatigable devotion to the notion of a "national university." Washington first publicly revealed his idea during the first annual message to Congress in 1790. During the address he spoke at length about *teaching* the people the value of their rights. He later wrote to Alexander Hamilton that a national university would be the means whereby "the youth from all parts of the United States might receive polish of Erudition in the Arts, Sciences, and Belles Lettres; and where those who were disposed to run a political course might . . . be instructed in the theory and principles."

This suggestion was not among the deliberations of Congress during the first years of Washington's presidency. Still, a national university remained in his thoughts. Washington opposed the prevailing attitude that youth had to "migrate" to foreign countries to receive education by supporting and encouraging the establishment of seminaries.

Washington made his next serious attempt to endow a national university in 1795. Disappointed by the dull reaction of Congress to his plan, Washington determined to vest 50 shares of stock in the Potomac Company given to him by the Virginia Legislature toward the establishment of a national university. Constrained by his personal oath not to accept any "pecuniary recompense" for service to his country, Washington had been holding this stock in trust since 1785. Washington even selected the site in the new "federal city" where the national university was to be built. Unfortunately, the successor to the Potomac Company failed and Washington's endowment was lost. The national university was never realized.

Another gift of stock – shares in the James River Company – fared better. In 1796, Washington chose Liberty Hall Academy located in the Shenandoah Valley to receive 100 shares of this stock valued at $20,000, also given to Washington by the Virginia Legislature and held in trust by him since 1785. Washington was inspired to make this donation by the trustees' belief in western expansion along the James River. This extraordinary gift saved the small school from certain financial ruin. The trustees promptly renamed the academy Washington College in honor of its benevolent patron. Amazingly, Washington's original endowment still pays a small portion, $3.91 in 1991, of each student's tuition.

By the time my great-grandfather Robert E. Lee arrived on the campus of Washington College in 1865, the severity of the Civil War years had dilapidated the struggling school beyond George Washington's munificent contribution.

General Robert E. Lee, flanked by his son General William H. F. "Rooney" Lee (left) and his aide Col. Walter Taylor (right) on the front porch of Lee's house in Richmond in April 1865, shortly after the surrender at Appomattox Court House. *Sarah Tracy Collection, Mount Vernon Ladies' Association.*

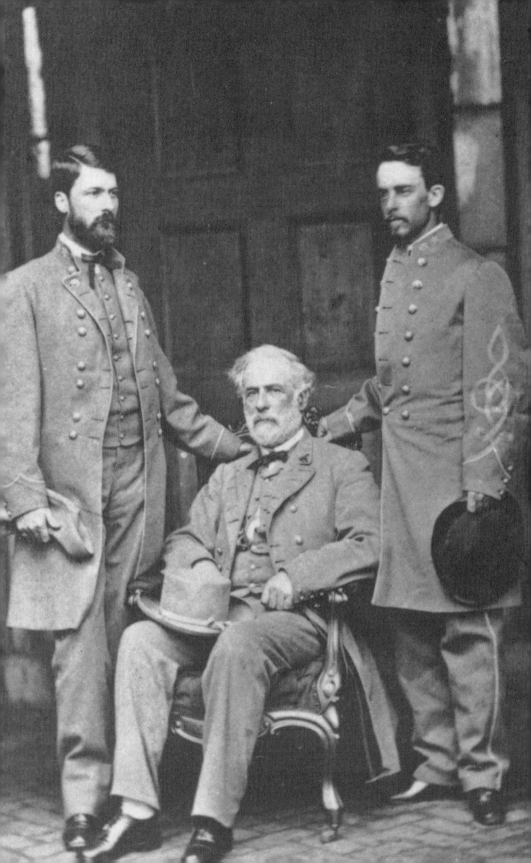

Robert E. Lee was one of many Americans who benefited from George Washington's unswerving and magnanimous commitment to education. Colleges sprang up throughout war-weary America during the first half of the 19th century, and an *American* education was becoming acceptable to middle-class families.

West Point was one such school, and it was to that military academy that Lee went in 1825. Robert E. Lee was one of several sons of the famous Revolutionary War hero Henry "Light-Horse Harry" Lee. Robert was born at Stratford Hall, only a few miles from the site of George Washington's birth. Robert's father had fought alongside Washington, but when the war ended, the absence of military challenge left him despondent, and he never achieved the glory hailed upon Washington. It was natural then that Robert pursued his education as a West Point cadet. As a student he excelled, finishing second in his class without a demerit. He studied diligently, particularly engineering, and he successfully used the skills he learned throughout his military career.

In 1852, Lee, now an officer in the United States Army, received unexpected orders assigning him to West Point as that school's superintendent. Lee reluctantly returned to his alma mater after his petition to be reassigned failed. Lee wanted to practice war, not teach it. He quietly and efficiently served his three-year tenure as superintendent before returning to the field with the Second Cavalry. Still, his brief tour of duty at West Point would have future implications in his choice of a career after the Civil War.

Lee fought brilliantly during the Civil War, but all too often in vain on the part of the Confederate states. Upon surrendering to General Ulysses Grant at Appomattox Court House in 1865, Lee's future suddenly became uncertain. He was determined that the South should rebuild itself, so he moved his family out of Richmond to nearby Derwent, where he intended to become a farmer. He had been there only a short time when Judge John Brokenbrough, representing Washington College in Lexington, Virginia, arrived offering him the position of president on behalf of the trustees of the school. At first Lee was skeptical, but he soon warmly embraced the notion.

Lee quickly adapted to the demands of his new profession. His brief tenure at West Point had prepared him to work with trustees, faculty, and students. Lee promptly unveiled his visionary plans of academic reform, to the delight of the trustees. He wanted to expand practical education by adding courses in scientific instruction. During the first years of his presidency, he proposed additional professorships and an enlarged curriculum featuring several schools or "departments" and elective courses. Lee was especially interested in agriculture, believing it to be the most important interest of the southern people.

In 1869, Lee introduced several innovative educational concepts, not previously known at any school in the country.

Lee proposed a "commercial school" to prepare students for business pursuits by teaching courses in commercial economy, trade, and mercantile law. Under Lee, Washington College became the first to envision a "school of journalism" by offering several "press scholarships." Students would be taught printing by a local publisher before becoming editors. Lee had other creative ideas, including graduate assistantships and a "school of Medicine and Pharmacy." Most of these ideas did not immediately flourish at Washington College. The institution was too small and isolated to embrace Lee's grandiose reform. He was accustomed to commanding an army of thousands; Washington College had only a few hundred students.

Lee died in October 1870, five years after accepting the presidency of Washington College. He was probably missed most by his students, all of whose names he was able to remember, to their great astonishment. While president of the college, Lee's reputation had caused many students to venerate the former general, and others to fear him. On one occasion, Lee expelled a student who appeared in his office chewing tobacco and refused to spit it out. Lee's belief in justice had helped to successfully transform the school into one of the two or three leading academic institutions of the South at the time of his death. To honor Lee, the college was later renamed Washington and Lee University.

Robert E. Lee's assumption of the presidential chair in 1865 was more than a new challenge, it was symbolic. The

memory of George Washington and Lee would be inextrica-
bly linked through their interest in and commitment to
education, embodied by the school that proudly bore their
names. Each man had done all that he could to promote
and encourage education in this country. For Washington
and for Lee, the war was over, but to their fruitful minds,
the American Revolution was just beginning.

DOROTHY TROTH MUIR

Presence of a Lady is another chapter in the history of Mount Vernon, the home of General George Washington, which stands high on the bank of the Potomac River in Virginia. It is the chapter that covers a seven-year period, beginning in 1861, when as the only national spot in a country torn apart by a War Between the States, ". . . removed from the scenes of conflict yet surrounded by them, so quiet itself that it seemed impossible the spirit of war could be hovering so near, yet within the sound of every gun, almost equidistant from the camps of the two armies, – this little corner of earth was kept sacred, neutral ground."

In 1853, the night boat had gone down the Potomac from Alexandria, carrying its usual crowd of travelers. About 10 miles below the city, the ship's bell began to toll dolefully. The boat went slowly past the Mount Vernon mansion. Ghostly, gaunt, and gray it stood, an ominous sight, enfolded in river mist, and lighted by the moon. Among the passengers was Mrs. Robert Cunningham of South Carolina, who had visited Mount Vernon when she was a child. Then it had been a stately white mansion, its lawn cut, and its shrubbery trimmed. She saw that unless something were done quickly, the famous old house would fall into ruins, its grounds overrun by brambles and briars. Yet who should take the responsibility of its care, she wondered. Suddenly she thought, it is the *women* of America who should repair and preserve Mount Vernon – mansion, grounds, and tomb.

When next she wrote to her invalid daughter, Ann Pamela Cunningham, she described the moonlit scene and expressed her own thoughts about the preservation of Mount Vernon. As Miss Cunningham finished reading her mother's letter, she exclaimed, "I will do it!" All of the strength and enthusiasm she had put into physical living, before a fall from her horse had made her an invalid, she put into planning a way to buy and maintain Mount Vernon. She wrote letters addressed to the "Women of America" and sent them to the newspaper. To these she initially signed herself "The Southern Matron." Through her untiring efforts she founded the Mount Vernon Ladies' Association, and became its first Regent. Brilliant, talented, sincere women stepped forward from each state to assist her and became the first Vice Regents. The owner, John Augustine Washington, Jr., agreed to sell the mansion and 202 surrounding acres for $200,000.

To arouse the public's interest in the undertaking, Currier & Ives, printmakers for the American people, issued a series of Mount Vernon views. *Harper's Monthly Magazine* printed an illustrated narrative by Benson J. Lossing, entitled "Mount Vernon As It Is." Mr. Godey ran the following statement in his popular *Lady's Book*: "There is no longer any reason to doubt the success of the plan for purchasing and preserving the home and grave of Washington. The present proprietor has acceded to the wishes of the Ladies' Association; and now we have only to raise the funds necessary to secure to the women of America this sacred spot. . . . Subscriptions and donations are received by the editors of the *Lady's Book*."

In June, 1859 when Miss Cunningham was in search of a good secretary, Sarah Tracy was introduced into the history of Mount Vernon.

5 Madison Square

Monday 20th

My dear Mr. Goodrich:*

Mrs. Gould and I have been considering the case of a secretary for Miss Cunningham.

Miss Sarah C. Tracy, formerly of Troy, New York, is now at Mr. James L. Grahams, No. 21 Washington Square. She is a special friend of ours. She is out of town, but will be there tomorrow morning. In every sense she would be just the person, and would, we think, accept the plan. Lady, both well educated and bright, agreeable, ready with her pen and her tongue. Every needed requisite.

---

*   ALSO KNOWN UNDER THE PEN NAME PETER PARLEY.

You will do a good thing for your friend, Miss Cunningham, and for our friend, Miss Tracy, if you can secure the services for one, and the place for the other.

Meanwhile, I wait for your letter. With kindest regards to the ladies,

Very truly yours,
Chas. Gould.

As a result of this letter, Miss Cunningham interviewed Sarah Tracy and engaged her as her secretary. She found that Miss Tracy was not only capable, but lovely to look at. Her clothes, which were the latest style, showed a decided French influence, Miss Tracy having lived for many years in New Orleans. She spoke both French and English. Although fashion decreed what Miss Tracy should wear, it never influenced the way she arranged her hair. She always parted it in the middle, and braided it in two heavy braids, which she coiled low over each ear.

A few months after Sarah Tracy became Miss Cunningham's secretary, the *Mount Vernon Record*, official organ of the Association, announced: "We are happy to see that the Regent is fulfilling her promise of carrying on the work of repairs at Mount Vernon as rapidly as possible. We noticed some time since, that through the kindness of Mr. Washington, workmen had been placed there under the superintendence of Mr. Upton H. Herbert, who is, by ancestry, closely allied with the history of Mount Vernon. His great-grandmother was a daughter of William Fairfax, and her sister married Lawrence Washington. . . . This connection makes the appointment of Mr. Herbert peculiarly appropriate, as from this fact he takes rather a personal pride in the place, and works *con amore*."

Mr. Herbert was a handsome man, well over 30, strongly built but not heavy. Service in the Mexican War had left a military squareness to his shoulders. His well shaped hands were at once languorous and alert, like the hands of his white–wigged ancestors who could pick up a lady's handkerchief or draw a sword with equal grace, and whose pictures adorned the walls of Virginia's best parlors. The men of Fairfax County liked and respected him. The women had considered him for the past 10 years one of the county's most eligible, though elusive, bachelors.

On February 22, 1860, John A. Washington and his family moved out of Mount Vernon, and the Mount Vernon Ladies' Association took possession of the mansion and the surrounding 202 acres. Except for the furniture that Mr. Herbert had brought from his own home and a few pieces left by John A. Washington, the house was empty. The work of repairing, furnishing, and then beautifying Mount Vernon lay ahead of the Ladies, and Miss Cunningham begged Mr. Herbert not to abandon his post as Superintendent in the event of war.

In the late fall of 1860, Miss Cunningham was called to her home in South Carolina. While she was gone, her young secretary was shopping for furniture, curtains, and carpets to make the Mount Vernon mansion a comfortable head-quarters for her when she returned. Miss Tracy kept the Regent constantly informed as to what she was doing. In one letter she wrote: "I have been all day buying. . . . I was frightened at the idea of daring to choose carpet and oil-cloth for Mount Vernon, but I did the best I could," and "shall I get a striped table cover, they are fashionable, or is it of no consequence?" At another time she wrote about Mount Vernon: "The house looks very much better than I anticipated, though some rooms are shabby enough, still we can make it very comfortable. I shall have to make some purchases in Alexandria. There are hardly any kitchen utensils at all, and an *absolute necessity* is window shades for the library, or curtains."

In March 1861, Miss Tracy was still expecting Miss Cunningham to return from South Carolina and go with her to Mount Vernon. Her letters, written to the Regent in the years that followed, are not only a vivid and human history of Mount Vernon during the War Between the States, but an unconscious character study of both herself and Mr. Herbert. She steps from the pages of her letters with all the quiet charm of a lady from Godey's *Lady's Book* and becomes an unforgettable personality as she writes: "I have found the troubles of today so absorbing as to annihilate those of yesterday, and those of tomorrow too far off to command attention."

ERNEST B. FURGURSON

If Abraham Lincoln had ordered any of his many commanding generals to lead the Army of the Potomac in a straight line from the District of Columbia to the Confederate capital of Richmond, his troops would have had to march directly across George Washington's plantation at Mount Vernon. Between April 1861 and April 1865, the Union army did everything but that.

Federal forces spent four years and thousands of lives striving to reach Richmond and end the Civil War. Moving by foot and horseback, barge and gunboat, they passed daily within yards of Washington's estate. The thunder of guns in major battles rolled over the old plantation. Southern cavalrymen repeatedly raided the fords and cross-roads that Washington himself had ridden when going to church and inspecting his outlying farms. Fleets of Federal transports shuttled up and down the Potomac River past his mansion house. Yet neither Yankees nor Rebels ever set a martial foot on the grounds of Mount Vernon.

No other such island of neutrality existed.

Mount Vernon was surrounded by the war, but those

who so bravely cared for it from 1861 to 1865 had only the sketchiest knowledge of what was happening that close at hand. Indeed, while it was going on, the common soldiers in the middle of those Civil War battles realized little of what happened beyond their own sight. They understood too well the drudgery of army life and the personal horrors of combat. But we today, with the perspective of time and immense documentation, can see the broad strokes of their war more clearly than they did.

Belatedly, the place where George Washington lived and was buried was revered by all Americans, North and South. But it was most special to Virginians – through their affection for Washington himself, and particularly, in 1861, through their respect for Robert E. Lee.

Lee's father, the rambunctious "Light Horse Harry," had been Washington's favorite cavalryman during the Revolution. As a congressman he had offered the resolution that designated Washington "first in war, first in peace, and first in the hearts of his countrymen." Young Robert Lee married the great–granddaughter of Martha Washington. They lived at Arlington, the mansion that Mrs. Lee inherited from her father, who had been raised as a son by Washington. Arlington was a virtual museum of Washington memorabilia brought from Mount Vernon; when Lee went off to the Mexican War, he dined in the field with Washington's silver, taken along as part of his kit.

In April 1861, Lee left Arlington for the last time, taking

the train to Richmond to accept command of Virginia's forces. There, the state's convention told him that "you are at this day, among the living citizens of Virginia, 'first in war.' We pray God most fervently that you may so conduct the operations committed to your charge, that it will soon be said of you, that you are 'first in peace,' and when that time comes you will have earned the still prouder distinction of being 'first in the hearts of your countrymen.'"

To Virginians, Lee was the Washington of his day, commanding forces committed not to rebellion, but to revolution – a distinction made honorable by the master of Mount Vernon.

But Mount Vernon was only 16 miles from Lincoln's White House, and a hundred from the capital of Virginia. Maryland, reluctantly loyal to the Federal government, possessed the broad Potomac. Thus the legal border between the Confederacy and the Union did not run half a mile away through mid-river, but literally by the foot of Mount Vernon's sloping lawn. And in the mid-1800s, Unionist Quakers from the North had bought many Fairfax County farms, including two of Washington's former plantations, adjoining Mount Vernon itself. For those who held Washington's home sacred, there was every reason to hold it neutral.

Even before Fort Sumter was fired upon, Gen. Winfield Scott, the U.S. general in chief, sent a company of Marines down to man crumbling Fort Washington, on the Maryland

shore just upriver from Mount Vernon. Till then the fort's
entire garrison had been "one old Irish pensioner . . .
General Scott said that it might easily have been taken by a
bottle of whiskey." Then, in mid–April of 1861, the fall of
Sumter set off celebrations in Virginia. Though the state
convention earlier had voted two to one against secession,
Lincoln's call for 75,000 troops to put down the rebellion in
the deep South reversed that decision.

That very day, April 17, the first Confederate flag went
up over Alexandria, eight miles from Mount Vernon and
within spyglass range of Lincoln's White House. James
Jackson, the defiant innkeeper who hoisted it, said it would
only be taken down over his dead body.

Before dawn on May 24, the morning after Virginia
voters ratified the convention's decision, heavy columns of
Union troops marched into Alexandria. The 24–year–old
colonel of the 11th New York Fire Zouaves, Elmer Ellsworth,
strode into Jackson's little hotel and yanked down the
offending flag. As he started down the stairs, Jackson
stopped him with a shotgun blast. Another Zouave immediately shot Jackson dead. Some said the blood of Jackson
and Ellsworth ran together on the stairway, a symbol of
what was ahead for North and South.

As Confederate militia withdrew ahead of the over–
whelming Union forces, neutral Mount Vernon briefly
anchored the line of demarcation between the two armies.
In late May of 1861, three Federal gunboats bombarded

Rebel forts at Aquia Creek, the Richmond, Fredericksburg and Potomac rail terminus about 20 miles downriver. In June, the 1st South Carolina Infantry ambushed a train carrying an Ohio regiment as it approached a station at Vienna, west of Alexandria. A pair of Rebel six-pounders blasted the train and scattered the Yankees. For the first time since 1814, the sound of artillery fired in anger drifted across the fields of Mount Vernon. Then in July, Union troops under Brig. Gen. Irvin McDowell started their first drive "on to Richmond."

Congressmen and ladies bearing parasols and opera glasses joined the crowd of light-hearted picnickers that followed, expecting to watch the army brush aside the impertinent Confederates along a creek called Bull Run. Brig. Gen. Gustave Toutant Beauregard, "the hero of Sumter," commanded the Rebel force defending the Manassas rail junction, some 20 miles west of Mount Vernon. Brig. Gen. Joseph E. Johnston rushed Confederate reinforcements forward.

Against a Union flanking movement, a quirky brigadier named Thomas J. Jackson formed a second line of defense. Brig. Gen. Barnard Bee galloped up to tell him, "General, they are driving us back!" – to which Jackson replied, "Then, sir, we will give them the bayonet." Turning to his broken regiments, Bee shouted, "Look! There is Jackson standing like a stone wall. Rally behind the Virginians!" – and one of the great legends of military history was born.

That Sunday, July 21, the concussion from the faraway guns shook the farmhouses of Fairfax County. Families whose sons were soldiers could only fearfully imagine what was happening.

Anne Frobel, of Wilton Hill near Alexandria, told her diary that "There was very little breakfast needed or consumed in this house today. The war of cannon was incessant from early dawn till after sunset and O such a day . . . the intense misery – the wearing anxiety of that day . . . . Sometimes when there would be an unusually loud burst – a volley loud and long I would stop and stand still, shut my eyes and clasp my hands – I could not pray . . . . My cry all day long was mercy – mercy – Lord have mercy . . . ."

Two days later, Frobel's servant came back from Alexandria and reported that he "seed a great many officers and men going off the boat into the City – and the whole town of Alex – and all the roads about wuz jis chuck full of soldiers . . . . All appeared to be in a very dilapidated condition, one man he saw sitting on the wharf looking very miserable, first he took off one shoe and then the other and poured blood out of them." Anne's sister, Lizzie Frobel, in a froth of curiosity, took a carriage into town and returned "With both hands uplifted, and beaming face. She exclaimed – O Nancy, Nancy, we have had the most *glorious victory* you ever heard of . . . ."

Thus, by word of mouth, news of Confederate success at First Manassas came to a countryside shut off from timely mail and newspapers. Most in Washington heard the bad news the same way. Then, when rumors rose that the victorious Southerners were marching on to the capital, Union officers mounted an aerial reconnaissance for the first time in America and proved the rumors wrong.

Soon after his inauguration, Lincoln had granted an audience to a venturous ex-cobbler from New Hampshire who styled himself "Professor" Thaddeus S.C. Lowe, a professional balloonist. Older generals scoffed at the idea that his observation balloons could be useful in war, but Lowe impressed the president by sending him the first telegraph message from the air. He was commissioned to create a balloon corps for the army.

In the near-panic after Manassas, Lowe took off on his first operational flight, from one of the forts that ringed Washington. Soaring over enemy lines, he then caught winds that brought him back to the Potomac. When surprised friendly troops fired at him, he climbed out of musket range and sailed on – and finally came down beyond Union control, on one of the Mason plantations above Mount Vernon. There he lay low until night, when his wife disguised herself as a farm woman and brought a covered wagon to rescue her husband and his deflated balloon.

That fall Lowe turned the former Washington–to–Mount Vernon steamer *George Washington Parke Custis* into the world's first aircraft carrier.

Ordered to scout Confederate defenses along the

Potomac, he planked over the vessel's deck and mounted on it his hydrogen–generating apparatus and launching gear. Chugging downriver past Mount Vernon, Lowe's rig operated off the mouth of Mattawoman Creek and gave Union officers a clear view of Rebel gun emplacements around Freestone Point, on Occoquan Bay. Lowe's success on the river won his balloon a vital role in the Peninsula and Chancellorsville campaigns ahead.

In late 1861, after the repulse at Manassas, Confederate and Union cavalry clashed six miles from Mount Vernon at Pohick Church, where Washington had been a vestryman. They collided again four miles away at Accotink, Mount Vernon's closest post office. Though these firefights were heard clearly and raised fears at the mansion, the only soldiers who came there still were peaceful sightseers.

Union Maj. Gen. George B. McClellan had decided that rather than trying again to drive overland to Richmond, the easier way was a great flanking movement, to strike up the Peninsula between the James and York rivers. To get there, he had to move most of his massive army down the Potomac to Chesapeake Bay.

One morning in early spring of 1862, Anne Frobel went to Alexandria "and found the whole world moving to Richmond. The Potomac River . . . as far as we could see was one solid mass of white canvas – You could only get a glimpse of the water here and there so thickly were the vessels – boats, steamers, little and big, of all sizes and shapes – crowded – crowded – packed together . . . . Under those circumstances I should have thought it a sight beautiful to look upon. But O what a sinking heart-sickness to remember the errand they are upon – and such an immence, immence army – how can our little band stand before it . . . God help them!"

For hours and days, this motley fleet hurried back and forth past Mount Vernon. When it was gone, another government steamer approached the dock at the foot of the lawn. President Lincoln brought his visiting sister-in-law and a party of Springfield folk to see Washington's home place. With Mrs. Lincoln and perhaps ten others aboard, their vessel stayed an hour and a half.

Lincoln had long realized the parallel between himself and Washington – men so different in background, both called by history to bring their country through crisis. Indeed, as he departed Springfield for Washington, Lincoln had said he faced "a task before me greater than that which rested upon Washington. Without the assistance of that Divine being who attended him, I cannot succeed. With that assistance I cannot fail."

Lincoln might have sought inspiration at Mount Vernon by standing at the tomb of Washington, remembering how 80 years earlier, one man's courage had sometimes seemed all that assured national survival. Indeed, Mrs. Lincoln had come there the previous spring, only three weeks after her husband's inauguration. But whether the president himself set foot ashore and toured the grounds is a lingering question: his biographer, Benjamin Thomas, suggests that he did, but some accounts say he remained aboard the boat. After all, he had heavy matters on his mind – that April 2 was the day McClellan arrived at Yorktown and started the Peninsula campaign. (Yet the most memorable item among the busy president's recorded personal papers for the day is a letter of thanks to Michael Crock of Philadelphia for sending a pair of white rabbits to Lincoln's son, "Tad.")

When McClellan moved on Richmond from the Chesapeake, the Confederates pulled their main army out of northeastern Virginia to reinforce the Peninsula. Not until after McClellan's offensive had been turned back by the new Confederate commanding general, R.E. Lee, did the Federals try again to drive on Richmond by land. The result was the second battle of Manassas, a tactical masterpiece in which Stonewall Jackson and James Longstreet's forces combined to defeat the boastful Union commander, John Pope.

Yet again, the mutter of cannon had the keepers of Mount Vernon wondering whether the war had turned their way. But this time, the victorious Lee struck northwestward into Maryland, to fight McClellan to a bloody draw on the fields along Antietam Creek.

The familiar cry of "On to Richmond!" rang again. The next Federal commander, Ambrose Burnside, chose the direct route to the Confederate capital. In December, he crossed the Rappahannock River and tried to ram through

Lee's army defending the heights behind Fredericksburg, 35 miles south of Mount Vernon. The waiting Rebels smashed waves of his infantry in one of the most lopsided fights of the war. Battered and hungry, the two armies dug in along the Rappahannock to wait out a winter that had 27 recorded snowfalls. But even as the foot soldiers shivered, Confederate horsemen kept Union forces in a state of nerves far behind the front lines.

At year's end, the flamboyant Jeb Stuart led some 1,800 cavalrymen with four cannon to cut rail lines north of the Occoquan River. He surprised the telegraph office at Burke Station, 10 miles from Mount Vernon and barely 14 from the White House. From there, he sent a message to Lincoln's quartermaster general, complaining about the quality of the Union mules he had been taking of late.

In the pre-dawn darkness of early March, John Mosby, the daring Confederate partisan, led a little band of riders through Union lines to the Federal command post at Fairfax Court House. Rousting a Yankee brigadier out of bed, he rode off with 31 prisoners and 58 fine horses. Lincoln, told of the loss, cracked, "Well, I am sorry for that, for I can make brigadier-generals, but I can't make horses."

But the president's sense of humor was buried when spring came. In an Easter snowstorm, he boated down the Potomac to Aquia Creek, then took a special train to visit his latest army commander, "Fighting Joe" Hooker, and hear his plan to take Richmond.

Hooker laid out a superb flanking maneuver – and in the last days of April 1863, he carried out its opening moves brilliantly. But then, at Chancellorsville, he collided with Lee and Jackson. In the war's most spectacular display of quick-thinking generalship, they drove Hooker's army back across the Rappahannock river. Head–on fighting produced 30,000 casualties, and for days afterward, boats bearing the dead and wounded crept in sad procession past Mount Vernon. In Washington, the poet and volunteer nurse Walt Whitman waited and watched:

You ought to see the scene of the wounded arriving at the landing here at the foot of Sixth Street, at night. Two boat-loads came about half-past seven . . . . A little after eight it rain'd a long and violent shower. The pale helpless soldiers had been debark'd, and lay around on the wharf and neighborhood anywhere . . . . The few torches light up the spectacle. All around – on the wharf, on the ground, out on side places – the men are lying on blankets, old quilts, etc., with bloody rags bound round their heads, arms, and legs . . . . The men, whatever their condition, lie there, and patiently wait till their turn comes to be taken up . . . . A few groans that cannot be suppress'd, and occasionally a scream of pain as they lift a man into the ambulance. To-day, as I write, hundreds more are expected, and to-morrow, and the next day, more, and so on for many days. Quite often they arrive at the rate of 1,000 a day.

Again Lee followed up success by moving north – this time to be halted at Gettysburg. After the bloodletting there, neither army would mount another major offensive for many months. When the Union army moved again in early May of 1864, a new and determined general named U.S. Grant was in charge.

Crossing the Rappahannock and Rapidan, Grant fought Lee at the Wilderness, then despite heavy losses moved on and fought again at Spotsylvania Court House. Keeping up the pressure on Lee's outnumbered army, Grant sideslipped southward only to be stopped in the slaughter pen of Cold Harbor. In his month–long drive to the outskirts of Richmond, the Union army alone suffered more than 50,000 casualties. All that late spring, the Potomac waterway and the dusty roads of northern Virginia were busy with ambulances and hearses heading north, and fresh troops heading south.

A rare reversal of that flow came in mid–July, when Maj. Gen. Jubal Early led an army of 14,000 Confederates in a looping raid through the Maryland countryside to come at Washington from the north. Early deployed his troops and advanced on Fort Stevens, at the far end of the capital's Seventh Street. With Lincoln in his stovepipe hat looking on, Federal artillery opened fire. Early halted, but his mission to divert Union strength from outside Richmond was at least partly successful: the veteran Sixth Corps rushed up the Potomac past Mount Vernon, and its timely arrival in the Washington fortifications convinced Early that he had done enough, so he withdrew.

The casualties would still flow back from Richmond and Petersburg. A few more times, Rebel raiders would dart and jab at key crossroads and supply points in Fairfax County. But neither Washington nor Mount Vernon would hear the guns of war again.

Late on Palm Sunday, April 9, 1865, the military telegraph brought news to Washington that triggered booming cannon salutes next morning, and celebrations that lasted into the night. Only later did those at George Washington's mansion downriver learn what that noise meant, when they heard of Lee's surrender at the obscure Virginia village of Appomattox Court House.

The fighting was nearly over, but not the trauma. Five days after Appomattox, John Wilkes Booth shot Lincoln at Ford's Theater. A great moan went up from millions of Americans, including many in the South. Booth hid from his pursuers in southern Maryland, beyond the Potomac, then made his way across to Virginia. There, in a blazing tobacco barn near Port Royal in Caroline County, Booth was fatally shot. From Belle Plain above Fredericksburg, his body was brought past Mount Vernon aboard the steamer *John S. Ide.*

The mournful epilogue to the nation's most dangerous years had closed. With peace, two boatloads of visitors started calling at Mount Vernon each day.

There, a lady from upstate New York and a man deeply rooted in Virginia had protected Washington's home from violation by North and South. They could take pride in what they had done, and we can take pleasure in this fascinating account of how they did it.

CHAPTER ONE

ONE

NATIONAL SPOT,

1 8 6 1

$\mathcal{S}$arah C. Tracy, secretary to the first Regent of the Mount Vernon Ladies' Association, drew a sheet of note paper toward her and began to write:

>Clarendon Hotel,
>March 13, 1861

My dear Miss Cunningham,

I think I wrote you last on Friday, we were then on the way of going to Mount Vernon, but it poured in such torrents on Saturday that no one could go. But the boat went down on Monday, which was a lovely day.

The place looked very sweet, though nothing more has been done about the mansion than painting the Portico and one side of the house. They are now at work on the other side. The windows have been washed, and a great deal of cleaning done — but there is plenty yet to be done. I could not see the half I wanted to attend to, there were so many people about. But Mr. Herbert informed me he had about $200 more than when we were there.

He wants permission to put General Washington's room in perfect order, that is plaster, paper and paint. He says that if the room had been in order he could have paid a man to guard it, and make money besides. One of the Lewises is about breaking up housekeeping and Mr. Herbert says he can get some chairs on deposit. In this way the room can be furnished and will pay. Mr. Herbert says the sills will last three or four years longer, but the roof cannot be longer delayed, it leaks badly and will injure the house. He wants permission to shingle.

The little porch by the library windows is coming down on itself. Would you like a plain narrow balcony, or platform-like, without a roof, or steps placed there temporarily until the rest of the house is finished, just for our accommodation It would not be expensive . . . .

Washington City,
March 28, 1861.

. . . I will go down on Saturday and tell Mr. Herbert about the room. The plastering is in some places very badly broken, but I thought that could be mended, unless on examination the lathes *are also decayed, and the room painted and then papering can be done at any time you and the Ladies think best . . . . You know a room can be papered at any time without injuring the paint.*

Did I write you that the wind carried away the covered passage from the house to the kitchen, and one side of Judge Washington's porch. I will tell you when I come back from Mount Vernon, but I imagine the roof can be temporarily supported, or removed and still the platform be left.

Mr. Graham went with me to Alexandria to inquire about the furniture there, and he thinks you could not get the same any cheaper in New York or Philadelphia. The man will make a single bedstead, a kind of French Bedstead, simple but rich for $14.00, a tufted, hair-cloth, mahogany chair, low, such as I think you would like, for $13.00, and like the one you saw in the Hotel parlor, a kind of rocking chair without rockers, for $30.00.

I could find but one place to inquire about curtains, etc., and the prices were absurd, but I have heard of another which I will go and write you the answers to all your other inquiries . . . .

The weather is very Marchy and disagreeable. I have a wretched cold in my head and have not been out since Monday, but if I had

---

First Lady Mary Todd Lincoln visited Mount Vernon in March 1861 with a group of friends. Sarah Tracy was away at the time, but resident superintendent Upton Herbert showed the party around the estate. This carte de visit of Mrs. Lincoln is from the personal collection of Sarah Tracy, now at Mount Vernon.
Sarah Tracy Collection, Mount Vernon Ladies' Association.

received your letter yesterday, I would have gone down to Mount Vernon today.

I have not seen Mrs. Lincoln, but unprejudiced persons say she is rather stout, dresses in admirable taste, and receives like a lady. Mrs. Berghman[1] saw her more than once, and said there was nothing coarse or unlady-like in her manner or conversation, all the slang and bad manners attributed to her is false.

On the following day, Miss Tracy wrote to Miss Cunningham again about Mrs. Abraham Lincoln:

. . . Soon after mailing my letter yesterday I heard that Mrs. Lincoln and party went down to Mount Vernon, on Tuesday, like anybody else. The enclosed clipping appeared in the Star.

Mrs. Lincoln, accompanied by Mr. and Mrs. Kellogg, of Illinois, and a select party of friends, paid a visit to Mount Vernon, per steamer Thos. Collyer, on Tuesday last. The party was escorted over the grounds by Captain Baker, of the Collyer, who contrived to make the trip an agreeable one to his distinguished guests in every respect.

April 1, 1861,

. . . Mr. Herbert was very polite to them, took them in the Banqueting room, and General Washington's room, and the gardens. His dinner was just ready, and he gave them a little lunch, of bread, butter and 'Ham.'" On the whole they had a very pleasant time.

1 VICE REGENT FOR PENNSYLVANIA.

In nearly every letter that Miss Tracy wrote there were a
few lines about the work that was being done on General
Washington's bedroom.

. . . *The paper is in places very badly discolored, but behind the
door there is a long piece which we thought with care could be
removed in long strips, at least two, if not three, so as to have them
for a pattern to decide upon other paper. But Mr. Herbert says the
plastering can be mended and the wood painted, and then the
windows can be altered and the room papered at any time.*

*I have seen the gentleman at the Patent Office who distributed
seeds and he is going to send us a quantity for Mount Vernon.*

Washington,
April 5, 1861

My dear Miss Cunningham,

*I was greatly relieved on my return from Mount Vernon yester-
day to receive yours of Saturday. . . . I am glad you are satisfied
on the subject of Mrs. Lincoln's visit. I enjoyed my visit there
very much. . . .*

*I found the house in good order, all the rooms have been swept
and cleaned. There was no trouble about the garret, the rooms look
quite tidy, and some of them habitable. I could not cut the carpet,
for the men were sanding the paint on that side of the house and
have closed the windows so tightly with their scaffolding that I
could not run the risk of doing it in the dark.*

*The vegetable garden is in fine order, green peas six inches high,
strawberries in blossoms, we had plenty of lettuce. The men have*

not quite finished the road yet, but in a week it must be done. They have been delayed by so much wet weather. It seems the contract only requires them to finish the road to its connection with the path leading to the old Tomb. All that bad piece from that point to the entrance to the lawn is to be left. True, it is a short distance, but it is as bad as any portion. But Mr. Herbert said that unless you said so of course he could not have it done at present. I told him I would write immediately and ask, for I did not believe but that you were of the same impression that I was, that the contract extended to the gate at the entrance of the barn yard. Between that and the lawn entrance, you will recollect, the road is paved. Would it not be better have it done now while the men are there with their carts and horses, than to have such a small piece unfinished? It would not take them but a few days, and the small piece is in such a conspicuous place.

Mr. Herbert says he has a black walnut extension dining table which you can borrow if you will. It will shut up so as to be just a good size for four persons. Do you not think you would prefer that to buying a new one?

I am sending you the enclosed notice to see if you would like me to get someone to buy half a dozen dining-room chairs. You know there are but four in all, and they are not alike and would be useful elsewhere . . . .

It was then that the war broke out, and though Upton Herbert remained at the mansion, the Ladies all felt that the greatest protection Mount Vernon could have would be the presence of a lady. Miss Cunningham sent an urgent message to Miss Tracy asking her to get a woman to chaperone her and to go at once to Mount Vernon.

> *Washington City*
> *April 13, 1861*
>
> *My dear Miss Cunningham,*
>
> *Yours of April 6th with Mrs. Ritchies[2] enclosed I have just received. The violent rains have so effected the roads that the mails South were detained several days. I am writing without the least idea that you will receive my letter, for I suppose the mails will be stopped.*
>
> *This war news has completely unnerved me. May God forgive the ring leaders and provokers of such evil, both sides! Heaven only can see the end. It cuts into my heart whichever way I look.*

Two days later a story appeared in the New York *Herald* that caused great excitement in Alexandria and Washington. It told that the body of General George Washington has been removed from his tomb and taken away to the mountains of Virginia.

Upon reading the article, Miss Tracy wrote at once to the *National Intelligencer*, Washington:

> *We are requested by the ladies of the Mount Vernon Association to state that the assertation which appeared in the New York Herald of the 15th instant to the effect that Col. J. A. Washington had caused the removal of the remains of General Washington*

---

2 VICE REGENT FOR VIRGINIA.

from Mount Vernon is utterly false and without foundation. *Never, since first laid in this his chosen resting place, have the remains of our Great Father reposed more quietly and peacefully than now, when all the outer world is distracted by warlike thoughts and deeds. And the public, the owners of this noble possession, need fear no molestation of this* one national spot *belonging alike to North and South. Over it there can be no dispute! No individual or individuals has the* right, *and surely none can have the inclination, to disturb this sacred deposit.*

The Ladies have taken every necessary precaution for the protection of the place, and their earnest desire is, that the public should feel confidence in their faithfulness to their trust, and believe that Mount Vernon is safe under the guardianship of the Ladies of the Mount Vernon Association of the Union.

The last week in April, Miss Tracy went to Alexandria and found it wild with excitement. She wrote to Miss Cunningham telling her of the long lines of refugees pouring in from Washington, and of her difficulty in finding a woman who was willing to accompany her to Mount Vernon, to be with her until her friend, Mary McMakin, should arrive from Philadelphia. She felt sure that she and Mary would be perfectly safe at Mount Vernon, in the midst of the rapidly approaching war, and added: "If Mr. Herbert is obliged to fight, and he may be, *we* will take care of Mount Vernon! Mr. Herbert has formed a Home Guard in the neighborhood."

Miss Cunningham wrote Miss Tracy that if Washington should become the seat of a terrible conflict, it might be well for Mr. Herbert to stop the Mount Vernon boat from running, in order to safeguard the mansion. Before he could take steps to stop the boat from running, however, the move was made unnecessary. The Government seized the *Thomas Collyer* and turned it into a troop transport. Miss Tracy notified Miss Cunningham of its seizure:

April 30, 1861

.... *Friday, received news of the attack on troops in Baltimore and determined to telegraph friends as to where I should go. Found the telegraph office in the possession of the Administration. Saturday and Sunday, days of intense excitement. Vessels laden with flour were seized, the flour carried to the Capitol for the use of Northern Troops. The Alexandria and Mount Vernon boats both seized.*

May 2, 1861

. . . *Mr. Herbert told the Captain of the Company of soldiers stationed near here your wishes with regard to their not coming here in uniform or armed. They have behaved very well about it. Many of them come from a great distance and have never been here, and have no clothes but their uniforms. They borrow shawls and cover up their buttons and leave their arms outside the enclosures, and never come but two or three at a time. That is as much as can be asked of them.*

Since the story of the removal of the remains, several persons, evidently Northerners, have been here, we suppose to see the truth of the story. They behave perfectly well, are quiet and gentleman-like.

Mr. Herbert felt it would be very wrong not to have any white man on the place but himself. He says the plan you speak of, that of making this a sort of refuge for those not at work, is impracticable, because every man out of employment who could be trusted has enlisted. Those who are left are not persons who ought to be trusted with Mount Vernon.

Mr. Herbert has resisted every tempting offer to join the Army. He has had several. Both his brothers, and every friend he has, have done so, and they wonder much that he has refused the command of every company offered. He says very little about it, but has, I know, made a sacrifice for Mount Vernon.

Alas, how sad all this makes us and what a change has come over the spirit of our dream.

When rumors began circulating through Virginia that Federal Troops might be placed at Mount Vernon, Miss Tracy took the omnibus from Alexandria to Washington. There she met her friend, Mr. Graham. Together they went through the excited crowds on the streets of Washington to the War Department to speak to Colonel Mansfield, who was an old friend of Mr. Graham's. When they were told the Colonel was out, Miss Tracy insisted on going straight to General Winfield Scott. At the door of the General's office, she found an officer whom she knew.

"I'm sorry," Major Townsend told her, "it will be impossible for the General to see you today."

"Just for a moment?" Miss Tracy begged, and explained why it was so important that she see him at once.

Unable to withstand her pleading, the Major opened the door and went over to the General's desk. Briefly he told General Scott of the neutral position that the Mount Vernon Ladies were attempting to maintain for Mount Vernon mansion.

Miss Tracy heard the General exclaim, "God bless the Ladies," and add something in a lower tone that she could not hear through the partly opened door. Major Townsend and a young officer with him were both laughing as they came out the door, but they grew serious at once, as they saw the anxious look on Miss Tracy's face.

"The General wishes me to assure you that no troops shall be placed at Mount Vernon under any plea what-soever," the Major told her kindly, "and asks if you can be equally sure of Virginia?"

And Miss Tracy, for the entire state of Virginia, un-hesitatingly answered, "Yes."

To Miss Cunningham she wrote:

. . . Mr. Graham thought it right that I should go to Mount Vernon at least for the present. He said that the presence of ladies there would be its greatest protection, even from the unruly. The expense will be less than elsewhere.

Dandridge and Emily are both dismissed. Priscilla and her sister will be all sufficient with a woman to come every week and wash. This arrangement will cost less than keeping the other three and if you are able to come and wish a man servant, then one can be hired as well as now.

Nothing is to be done except the work that two men can accomplish. Mr. Herbert considers the presence of two white men necessary to the protection of the place, and they will be sufficient. . . .

CHAPTER TWO

MOUNT VERNON

ON THE POTOMAC,

1 8 6 1

Twilight had fallen at Mount Vernon. A mist was hanging low over the Potomac, and from the marshes, to the west of the mansion, came the soft continuous sound of the peepers.

Within the mansion, dinner was over. There had been only Miss Tracy, Mr. Herbert's aunt, who was acting as her chaperone, and Upton Herbert at the table in the large family dining room where George and Martha Washington had entertained their family and friends for so many years. Now the room was empty. The servants had returned, by the covered way, to the kitchen and their quarters.

Miss Tracy went into the library, where the candles had already been lighted. The light shone on the empty shelves that had once held George Washington's books. It flickered on the large globe of the world and lighted Houdon's bust of Washington, which three generations of Washingtons had left standing high on the shelf where the General himself had placed it. It glowed on the turkey-red curtains drawn close across the windows. It shone warmly on Miss Tracy as she seated herself at the writing table. Slowly dipping her pen, she began to write her first letter to Miss Cunningham from Mount Vernon.

Mount Vernon,

May 11, 1861

Dear Miss Cunningham,

I wish you were here. Everything is so beautiful and peaceful one cannot realize that at so short a distance from us men's passions are driving them to all that is wicked and horrible.

Mother earth promises bountiful supplies from her store house to keep us from want, even if the foreign luxuries are cut off. We are eating delicious asparagus. The strawberry vines and fruit trees are laden. On the trees the fruit seems thicker than the leaves. But sugar and coffee we must go without. That will be pleasant!

A few days later, Upton Herbert wrote from the mansion:

Mount Vernon,
May 16th

Miss Cunningham,
Regent of the M.V.L.A.
Dear Madam,

I had the honor of receiving your letter on the 12th inst. All of your suggestions, in regard to the preservation and protection of Mount Vernon, shall be attended to. Miss Tracy will have informed you, ere this, of her interview with the powers that be at Washington. If you have sufficient confidence in my judgment in the matter, I think I can influence the soldiers of the Confederate Army, by stating to them your wishes, in regard to their visiting at Mount Vernon: but as it is your wish, I will see Colonel Terrett, who commands the troops in this vicinity, also.

The bedroom of General Washington has been replastered and painted. The leaks in the roof have been stopped; so that it will not be necessary, at this time, to reroof.

Mr. Riggs[3] has informed me that I must discharge the workmen, as there is no money now to defray the expense of keeping them.

Mr. Washington's farm houses are too far away to be injured by guns from the fort.

Respectfully yours,
U. H. Herbert

A week after this letter was written, the Northern Army, under cover of darkness, crossed the Potomac and seized the Southern city of Alexandria. Most of the Southern

---

3   GEORGE WASHINGTON RIGGS, PROMINENT WASHINGTON BANKER AND TREASURER OF THE MOUNT VERNON LADIES' ASSOCIATION.

soldiers in the city were warned in time to escape, however, and reassemble near Manassas Junction in Virginia. Arlington, the home of General Robert E. Lee, was also captured by the Northerners. General Lee had married Mary Ann Randolph Custis, the daughter of George Washington Parke Custis, who was the grandson of Martha Washington. Arlington and all that the mansion contained became Mary Ann's property at the death of her father. The house was filled with furniture, china, and ornaments that had once belonged to George and Martha Washington. When Mrs. Lee heard that Northern soldiers were marching toward Arlington, she ordered a large farm wagon driven up to the front door. On it she had piled as much of the treasured furniture as the vehicle would hold. Sorrowfully she took one last look at things she must leave. Then getting into her carriage, she drove swiftly away from her beloved home, the farm wagon following her down the long road into Virginia.

After the Union troops took Alexandria, mail service for the Mount Vernon neighborhood was discontinued. The little United States Post Office at Accotink was too far inside the Confederate line to have any contact with Alexandria or Washington and was too far north to be given Southern Postal Service. Letters had to be carried by special messenger either to Alexandria on the north or below Occoquan on the south. Miss Tracy wrote to Miss Cunningham, who was still in South Carolina, concerning the situation.

> *Mount Vernon,*
>
> *June 6, 1861*
>
> *. . . We are hoping for a Post Office at Occoquan, eight miles from here. . . . Roof leaking terribly again. We heard all the firing at the time of the attack on Aquia Creek. . . . It is fortunate that I am here, for from no other place, I know, could I communicate both ways.*

The possibility of her communicating both ways must have occurred to some of the military men in Washington, for Miss Tracy found that her letters had been suddenly stopped.

> *Mount Vernon,*
>
> *June 8, 1861*
>
> *. . . There is no Southern communication with Alexandria, and our letters are suddenly stopped. I may be able to send you a letter occasionally. You had better write me by way of Kentucky. We will try to get your box (of summer clothes) to you, if Mr. Herbert has to send it, as you say, to Manassas Junction.*
>
> *Colonel Stone, brother of Dr. Stone of Washington, is in command of the Federal forces at Alexandria. He is very gentleman-like and courteous; says not a soldier shall come here. He gives passes to our servants at our request. Mount Vernon and the Association are talismanic words.*

Miss Tracy made a trip to Washington, to the War Department, to ask permission to send letters from Mount

Vernon to Miss Cunningham. Her request was granted.

"But remember", Colonel Townsend caution~ ` ` :r, "not to say anything of a military nature in your lett~

Miss Tracy promised to remember, and noted as she was doing so, that the Major had been promoted to Colonel.

On June 17th, she wrote to Miss Cunningham:

I am known as a Northerner, and Mr. Herbert as a Virginian. . . . Mr. Herbert was advised not to go to Alexandria again. He had decided not to before, for he would not risk being examined and asked to take the oath. I went to town and got passes and saw Mr. Burke.

Washington and Alexandria are military cities. The entire outskirts are one great camp grounds. It is strange how quiet it is within these grounds; though we hear firing outside occasionally.

The servant, Dandridge, who Mr. Herbert had felt he must dismiss six months before in order to cut down expenses, had returned to the familiar security of Mount Vernon. Miss Tracy was given a Federal pass for him which read:

Hd 2nd Alexa Brigade,
Alexandria, June 29th, 1861
Pass Dandridge Smith (colored) with wagon, Mules, and Provisions for the Mount Vernon Association, in and out of Alexandria daily.

By order of Colonel Heintzelman

In 1859, Sarah Tracy of Troy, New York, accepted a position as secretary to Ann Pamela
Cunningham, founder and first Regent of the Mount Vernon Ladies' Association.
She lived in George Washington's historic Mansion throughout the Civil War and is credited
with preserving Mount Vernon during this period of national turmoil.
Mount Vernon Ladies' Association.

July commenced quietly, but the second week of July found the neighborhood wild with excitement. The Confederates had proclaimed July 15 as Muster Day, and many men who did not wish to be drafted unwillingly into the Southern Army were attempting to reach the outposts of the Northern Troops. The religious principles of the Quakers[4] in the Mount Vernon neighborhood were being respected by the Confederates, but there was scarcely a Friends' household that did not have one young son in a gray uniform, while a few miles away another son was wearing a blue one. The Quakers were to suffer not only the hardships of war, but the tragedy of divided loyalty.

The Friends, who had fled to New Jersey at the outbreak of the war, had nearly all returned. The large house on Union Farm,[5] about a half mile from Mount Vernon's West Gate, had been opened, and farther down the road, there were lights in Walnut Hill.[6] On Muster Day a group of Northern officers had dinner near Mount Vernon at Hollin Hall.[7] They had gone down to Mount Vernon and returned, without mishap, while in the same neighborhood a Southern Army was being mustered; so strangely was Mount Vernon situated during the war.

Miss Tracy mentioned the officer's visit in a letter to Miss Cunningham.

---

4   SEE *POTOMAC INTERLUDE* BY DOROTHY TROTH MUIR.
5   HOME OF JOHN BALLINGER.
6   HOME OF DAVID WALTON.
7   BUILT BY THOMSON MASON BUT OWNED AFTER 1852 BY EDWARD C. GIBBS.

July 15, 1861

. . . Occasional visits by troops, but we do not make much money. Today, officers called and gave me $6.50. Very little keeps us going.

To Mrs. Comegys, Vice Regent for Delaware, she wrote:

. . . I shall now remain here as long as it may seem best for the sake of Mount Vernon. I am glad I have remained, though, for my own sake, I have wished a thousand times that I was in China!

Saturday night I was horrified beyond measure at the receipt of letters from my friends, enclosing papers with General Beauregard, via Mount Vernon . . . . The only correspondence from Mount Vernon to the South are letters to Miss Cunningham, and a very neutral place it would be, if the Regent cannot be permitted to hear what is going on here!

True to her promise to Colonel Townsend, her letters South contained no military secrets, as she wrote:

. . . I am glad you say the roof may be shingled, for it is very necessary. Everything is very sweet about here, and I have had enough scrubbing and window washing done to keep the house in order.

Mount Vernon,
July 1861

. . . Before this letter reaches you, you will have the news of the terrible fight at Bull Run.

I have considerable strength of mind, but it was tried to the utmost yesterday. The wind was south on Thursday and we did not hear much of the firing till late in the afternoon, when for two hours, it was very distinct. But yesterday we will none of us forget!

At six o'clock in the morning, I was aroused by cannon, and from then till one o'clock there was not three minutes, no hardly one minute between firings. Then, for half an hour, it ceased; recommencing and continuing with equal rapidity til six o'clock, when there was over an hour's cessation. Then it commenced again and continuing til dark.

After the Battle of Bull Run, life within the grounds at Mount Vernon slowly returned to normal again. In the fields the corn stood straight and tall. Outside the open windows of the mansion, the locusts warned of hotter weather to come. Then suddenly, shattering the calm, the following order appeared.

Headquarters of the Army
Washington, D.C.
July 31, 1861

General Order No. 13

It has been the prayer of every patriot that the tramp and din of Civil War might at least spare the precincts within which repose the remains of the Father of this Country, but this pious hope is disappointed. Mount Vernon, so recently consecrated to the Immortal Washington by the Ladies of America, has been overrun by bands of rebels, who, having trampled under foot the Constitution of the United States, the ark of our freedom and prosperity, are prepared to tramp on the ashes of him to whom we are all mainly indebted for these mighty blessings.

Should the operations of our war take the United States troops in that direction, the General Officer does not doubt that every man will approach with due reverence, and leave undisturbed, not only the Tomb, but also the house, groves and walks which were so loved by the best and greatest of men.

By Command Winfield Scott

E. D. Townsend

Asst. Adj. General

As quickly as possible, Miss Tracy took up her pen and wrote a letter to the newspaper:

Messrs. Editors:

The officers of the Mount Vernon Association are pained to see, in your issue of today, an order from Lieutenant-General Scott containing a statement which they fear will lead to much trouble and misunderstanding, — General Scott having been misinformed as to the facts.

The statement referred to is that Mount Vernon has been 'over-run by bands of rebels.' Since the occupation of Alexandria by Federal troops not a single soldier from the Southern Army has visited Mount Vernon.

It is but justice to say that the intruders who refused to accede

to the regulations of the Association, heretofore willingly followed
by the soldiers from both sides, were a company of New York
Volunteers, headed by their Colonel and other officers.

The Regent is earnest and decided in her request and direction to
those she has made responsible for the preservation of order and
neutrality at Mount Vernon and in the discharge of this sacred
duty they have been kindly aided by those at Headquarters of the
Army. It is, therefore, to them a source of great regret to be obliged
to correct such a mistake; as it is much easier to excite than to allay
unkind feelings.

From Washington, Miss Tracy wrote to Mrs. Comegys,
on the same subject.

. . . I am here on another visit to General Scott. Some time since
a volunteer company came to Mount Vernon, about one hundred
and fifty. They had some hesitation about stacking their arms, but
finally consented and behaved very well. We were annoyed at so
many being in the grounds; but hoping it would not occur again,
said nothing.

A few days before the battle of Bull Run another large body of
men came down and refused to stack their arms, but were for over
an hour straggling all over the place without any order, their guns
in their hands. The Colonel said that if the men were to lay down
their arms, we must have an order to that effect from General Scott.

I wrote to Colonel Townsend, but before I sent my letter, heard
of the first battle of Bull Run, and concluded it would be better to

wait until the excitement was over, and it would be more likely to have proper attention. Then followed the second battle. I decided to wait until all was quiet and go myself. I found it necessary to have a pass signed by General Scott, himself. I saw Colonel Townsend. He said I should have all I wanted. I received a pass and a written order, signed by General Scott, to show any of his officers who do not wish to obey our regulations.

CHAPTER THREE

THE VISIT OF

PRINCE NAPOLEON

Life within the grounds at Mount Vernon continued quiet and peaceful. The seeds that Miss Tracy had planted in the old–fashioned flower gardens had grown well and were a riot of colors. Beside the gardens, the ruins of George Washington's greenhouse, which had burned nearly 30 years before, were almost entirely covered with vines, the tall chimneys standing like sentinels at each end. Shining, dark green vinca encircled the ground around the tall trees near the mansion; and in the twilight, the fireflies, gathering by the thousands in the trees; tall branches, blinked rhythmically against the evening sky. In the marshes, where the peepers had sung in the springtime, the hollow–voiced frogs croaked dismally. The coves of the river were filled with

large yellow and white water lilies, and the wild grape
vines, at the water's edge, promised an abundant harvest.

Mount Vernon Mansion,
August 13, 1861

But I must tell you of the visit of Prince Napoleon. When I left
Washington, he was expected there that evening, and I asked Mrs.
Riggs if she would come down and help me to receive him if he
came here. She said she would. Monday I sent to town for some
groceries I had purchased and some Claret Wine that had just
arrived from New York, as I was ordered to drink it. Thinking that
the party might come at any time, I had given directions to have
the house put in order, I had gone, and many things had been
neglected. Tuesday morning I was in the second story when I heard
a loud rapping at the door. Priscilla came and said there was a
large party of soldiers in citizens dress at the door. I heard them
walking about with Mr. Herbert, but took no notice of it until hap-
pening to be by a window as they passed out. I heard them convers-
ing in French. I looked out and heard enough to satisfy me whol-
ly. I waited until they had, as I supposed, all gone to the Tomb,
then rushed down stairs to make some Lemonade, open a box of
Claret, (so thankful *it had arrived, for you know, to a Frenchman*
it is essential). Priscilla had just arranged the waiter and I was in
the pantry making my Lemonade. I wanted something from the
sideboard and came into the dining room, to find myself face to face
with two gentlemen! I started and bowed, they likewise. I made
some remark about the heat, they looked blank, bowed, and shook

The surprise visit in August 1861 of Prince Napoleon, accompanied by the French minister
Count Mercier, was a highlight of the summer. Sarah Tracy hurriedly arranged a meal for the
guests and was able to communicate with them in their native tongue.
Sarah Tracy Collection, Mount Vernon Ladies' Association.

their heads. I repeated my remark in French, asking them if they
would have something. This opened their eyes and hearts, and
loosed their tongues. I soon found by the questions they asked

about a near village Hotel, that there was some cause of embarrass-
ment. I then asked one of them to please tell me frankly their trouble and if I could relieve them I would. It seemed there was a party
of seven, the Prince and five of his suite and Count Mercier the
French Minister at W—, they had left Washington at six o'clock (it
was ten when they arrived) without any breakfast, thinking they
could get some on the road. They had a driver who did not know
the road, probably because of the changes, — they had been provided
with such miserable horses they knew they could not return with
them, and they were anxious to have them cared for, and to find
others. I told them how we were situated, and how simply we were
living, but if I might be permitted, I would order the best breakfast
we could give them trusting they would excuse anything that was
wanting. They were full of thanks, feared the Prince would be
annoyed, but also feared he might suffer, they had no idea of
imposing upon us. I immediately set everybody to work and
ordered everything we had to be cooked, and then the party
returned from the Tomb! Breakfast, or rather lunch, was fairly
under way. The Prince told me the President offered him a steam-
boat which he declined, then, if he would come by land, a bully
guard of a hundred men. This he also declined preferring to come
without parade. They ate like hungry men and seemed to enjoy the
freedom from restraint and ceremony. I will make you laugh some-
day at some inconsistencies which agonized me at the time. They
remained till four o'clock. We sent a man with them to show them
around and in fifteen minutes he came back to get the mules, — one
pair of horses had given out. They were sent, and Prince Napoleon

rode to Alexandria in a carriage drawn by the Association mules! At Alexandria they procured fresh horses to Washington.

The Prince is a man of pleasant features, slightly Napoleonic, — mild expression, quiet gentleman-like manners, soft low voice, rather grave in its tone, but a merry laugh that sounds honest. He speaks English exceedingly well. The gentlemen of his suite were all very pleasant, varying enough to make the party agreeable. After lunch, I saw that it was entirely too hot for them to think of leaving, and after much persuasion, the Prince, who was evidently very weary, consented to try a little sleep on your bed. He slept for half an hour and was another man.

They were all much interested in the place and the Association, made many inquiries about you, seemed perfectly familiar with General Washington's history. The Prince was deeply impressed with the peculiarity of the position of Mount Vernon at this time, removed from the scenes of conflict, yet surrounded by them, — so quiet itself that it seemed impossible the spirit of war could be hovering so near, yet within the sound of every gun, almost equidistant from the camps of the two armies, yet this little corner of earth was kept sacred, neutral ground! He said it was a fact by itself in the history of the World, and the wars of the world, and he sincerely hoped we would be able to keep it so to the end! And I am sure all will echo that prayer.

To one of the Vice Regents, she wrote on the same subject.

.

On Tuesday we were surprised by the arrival of Prince Napoleon and his suite, accompanied by Count Mercier. They came down privately. We gave them the best we had, and they stayed from ten till four. They went over the place, and seemed much interested; were perfectly familiar with the history of General Washington, and much impressed with the neutral position of Mount Vernon, — hoped it would continue. Such a fact was unknown in history.

He is very pleasant, mild, refined of manner; a soft low voice, a merry laugh, and an earnest look that is pleasing. He speaks English very well, all the rest only French; so I was forced to gather up my half-forgotten ways and chat with them in their own tongue. They were all pleasant and agreeable. . . .

The Regent, Miss Cunningham, is in Greenwood, S.C., a place more elevated then her home, Rosemont. She is not well and is dispirited. Send your letters for her to me. I have a messenger who brings my letters form the Occoquan Post Office, and takes them there for me. I always put United States stamps on them and give him the money to pay for Southern Postage, and furnish him with stamps for those he takes from the Office so he cannot be compromised. I have also given him a written request to all soldiers to let him pass unmolested, as I have General Scott's sanction for my correspondence, and will be responsible for my messenger. He is a young man who worked here a long time as carpenter, and carries the letters without compensation, for love, declining any compensation. He frequently walks the nine miles and back. I always send once a week.

I had a curious adventure the night I left Washington. I have a pass from General Scott permitting me to pass the lines "at all times" and recommending me to "the courtesy of the troops." When I reached Alexandria, I found that the man had come for me, as I requested, the previous day, but not finding me, had left the horse and buggy and returned. I wanted to hire someone to drive me, but a friend persuaded me to take his nephew, a lad of fourteen. The orders were to let no one pass after five o'clock; but, armed with my pass, I was not in the least annoyed to find it a quarter past five before I left.

We passed the camp without difficulty, and were three miles on the road when we found the crossing barricaded. We came back the three miles and took another road. After going a short distance, we met a large body of troops at a turn in the road where there had never been any before. Instead of a sentinel, an officer came forward and said he was sorry I could go no farther that night. I showed him my pass. He pointed in another direction, and said that after going a short distance I would find the road barricaded, but by crossing a field I would come to a road through the woods, which would eventually bring me to the right road. I seemed literally "going round Robin Hood's barn," but we went on. Before quite reaching the barricade we were stopped by more troops. The captain said it was impossible. But I would go on! I told him what the other officer had said. He did not believe there was such a road, but would I allow him to see my pass. He read it and said, that would take me anywhere it was possible to go, but he had not heard of such a road. A little sergeant who was standing by asked if he might go and see. The captain said, "yes," and I waited.

Think of waiting at night among soldiers and barricades still six or eight miles from Mount Vernon.

I waited. Presently my friend returned and said there was a road but a bad one. I said I would try it. My little sergeant acted as a guide through the field, took down the bar, and let us into the woods. It was a pretty little road, narrow, and the trees lowering their branches to greet us as we passed. We two went on, without the most distant idea where the road would take us, but we continued until we found ourselves at the back entrance to a gentleman's farm. We passed through till, reaching the house, I sent John in to inquire if we might pass through to the road. The gentleman was very kind; said he feared our troubles were not over, but if we could not get through he would be happy to accommodate us for the night.

Another short drive, another body of troops, an officer more decided than the rest. He could not let us by. I showed him my pass.

He said, "That's all right, but if I allow you to pass by here, some of my men are farther on, with positive orders to let no one go by. Not to look at a pass, and to shoot anyone who resisted."

They were Poles, and I did not believe they would shoot a woman, but I asked him to send a soldier with me. He did so, and we passed them without a word! We turned into the Mount Vernon road and I felt safe. I said, "Now, drive fast, John, for it is getting late." When lo! another barricade, more formidable than the rest. The road was narrow, and so situated that there seemed no outlet but over a high fence or the tops of the trees! This latter I knew the horse would object to, for he was already showing sign of mistrust in the vagaries of one who generally allowed him to trot along home on a regular road. The fence I could not try alone; so John went back to ask the lieutenant to allow a couple of his men to come and open the fence. He came himself, with five men, examined the fence, and said it was so thoroughly made that it could not be taken down without cutting, which they were forbidden to do.

The men walked all around to see, and finally said there was a little gate. They would lead the horse through and lift the buggy over the fence, if they found I could get out the other side. I told them I must go on. If once around the barricade, I could reach the blacksmith's whose children worked at Mount Vernon, and I could leave the horse and buggy with him until morning, and could walk the rest of the way, the blacksmith knowing the paths through the woods.

One of the soldiers came to me and said that I had better not attempt it with only that lad. I asked him if there were more troops on the road. He said there were some of their men farther on, and some of another regiment that they could not be answerable for. The others returned and said there was no chance of getting out that way, but if I would stay all night at the gentleman's house nearby, they would help.

The gathering darkness was a unanswerable argument; so I did what I disliked, — turned my horse's head and begged a night's lodging at the house before whose gates these soldiers were stationed. While waiting to gain entrance, the lieutenant told me they had received information which made them expect an attack any minute, and he was glad I was not on the road. They had been cutting trees for four days to stop the cavalry from passing. I did not tell him what nonsense I thought it, nor how little I believed in the danger.

I was very comfortably lodged and slept soundly; though when I saw their arms glittering through the trees, I thought that if there should be an attack, it would be pleasanter to be somewhere else!

In the morning the Captain came to say his men had found a way for me to get around, and we once more commenced our "winding way." We went to another farm where there were two soldiers waiting to show us. We came into the road, and they said a little farther on we would find the last barricade, and some soldiers who would show us the way "round." This we reached in safety and found three soldiers, who took down a fence and led us through bush and briar, down a hill, over a ditch, through the fence, and congratulated us on being in a clear road. I assure you I was thankful.

M I S S   T R A C Y

A N D   T H E   B O N D S

When the Federal troops took Alexandria, the money and bonds that had been paid by the Mount Vernon Ladies' Association to John A. Washington were in a safe in Burke & Herbert's Bank.[8] An order was sent out from Headquarters that the money was to be confiscated. One morning a Northern officer, with a few men, entered the bank and demanded the Washington money. The man in charge of the bank told the searching party he knew nothing about the safe, that Mr. Burke was out of the bank at the moment, and Colonel Arthur Herbert[9] was with the Confederate Army. The officer and his men left the bank, planning to return when they could talk to Mr. Burke.

8   THIS STORY TOLD BY THE LATE MR. CHARLES H. CALLAHAN OF ALEXANDRIA TO THE WRITER.
9   BROTHER OF UPTON HERBERT.

They had no sooner left, than Mr. Burke returned and was told of their visit. He opened the safe, took out the money and bonds, and leaving the bank made his way quickly to his own home. When he reached the house, he found that Mrs. Burke had gone out for a drive, and the servants were busy in the back of the house. He went to his own room and opened the door of a large mahogany wardrobe that stood in the corner. He placed the package containing the bonds and money inside and pulled down some clothing in an untidy fashion; so that it was entirely hidden. Then he hurried back to the bank.

Just after he entered he heard the soldiers returning. It took him some time to convince the searchers that the money was not in the safe, nor in the bank. They realized that in some way they had been tricked, and, when at length they left the bank, they went directly to Mr. Burke's house. The officer in charge insisted on speaking to Mrs. Burke, who had just returned from her drive, and knew nothing about the package hidden away on the floor of the wardrobe. Annoyed because of the time he had already spent on his futile mission, the officer ordered a search be made. The house was ransacked from basement to attic. Bureau drawers were turned over, and Mr. Burke's private papers shuffled through in his desk. Only the wardrobe escaped careful scrutiny. Unable to find what he had been sent for, the officer and his men withdrew with promises to return.

As soon as word reached the bank that Union soldiers
had carried out an unsuccessful search of his house, Mr.
Burke quietly left the bank. The once pleasant streets of
the aristocratic old city were overcrowded with hurrying
soldiers and civilians from the North. He walked unnoticed
along the brick pavement. He had set out to find a man
whom he knew he could trust, a carpenter by trade.
Fortunately the carpenter was in his shop. The two men
made their way as inconspicuously as possible from the
carpenter shop to Mr. Burke's home. They went upstairs to
the bedroom where the money was hidden. Having made
their plans on the walk over, the carpenter began at once,
with swift skillful hands, to lift one of the wide boards from
the floor of the hallway outside of the bedroom door. Mr.
Burke went over to the wardrobe for the money and bonds.
As soon as the board was lifted, he dropped the package
into the opening beneath, and the board was returned to its
original position. For a few moments the carpenter worked
over it, and when he finally stood up both men felt satisfied
that the floor board was not in the least conspicuous.

General Winfield Scott, general in chief of the Union Armies at the beginning of
the Civil War, personally assured Sarah Tracy that no Federal troops would be placed at
Mount Vernon and its neutrality would be preserved.
Sarah Tracy Collection, Mount Vernon Ladies' Association.

The following morning, another searching party knocked at Mr. Burke's door. This time the officer was a gentlemanly young man, who apologize for having to search the house.

"It doesn't seem right to me," said Mrs. Burke, "that the great granddaughter of one of the Presidents of the United States should be obliged to accept such indignities at the hands of her countrymen." Martha Burke, who had been born at Monticello, was the great-granddaughter of Thomas Jefferson.

"No, it doesn't seem right," agreed the young officer, "and we shall try to cause you the least annoyance possible."

True to his word, he was as quiet and courteous as the officer on the previous day had been noisy and rude. Nevertheless the searchers were thorough, even the wardrobe was searched. And all the while that the search was going on, in the hallway beneath the continuous tread of polished boots, the package of bonds and money lay carefully hidden.

The following day, Miss Tracy drove out the long road from Mount Vernon mansion. No one could accompany her any longer. Mr. Herbert, a devout Southerner, had no pass through the Federal lines. Up the colonial road to Gum Springs she went, and then for five miles through scattered groups of soldiers and camps. Some days she drove to Alexandria with a load of cabbage for the city market, a menial task which she did proudly in order to raise additional funds to take of repairs at Mount Vernon. On this day she was taking a basket of fresh eggs.

When she reached Alexandria, she called at the home of her friends, Mr. and Mrs. John W. Burke. After she had been seated for a few moments, Mr. Burke asked, "Would you be willing to do a great favor for the Washington family?"

"I will do anything for them that is within my power," she replied without hesitation.

In a low tone, Mr. Burke told her what he would like to have her do, and then left the room to get the package for her. Miss Tracy sat for a moment deep in thought, then removing the eggs from her basket into her lap. Mrs. Burke silently nodded her approval. When Mr. Burke returned, Miss Tracy motioned him to place the package in the bottom of her empty basket.[10] Carefully replacing the eggs, she put the basket on her arm and said goodbye.

Seated in her little spring wagon, her basket of eggs on the seat beside her, Miss Tracy looked as lovely and helpless as a lady from Godey's *Lady's Book*. She rode down the streets of Alexandria, past some 75,000 Union soldiers, and armed with her Federal pass, crossed over the bridge, and entered the City of Washington. She drove directly to Mr. Riggs' office in the bank, rented a safety deposit box, placed the package of money and bonds inside, and locked the box. Then with a brief explanation and farewell to Mr. Riggs, she drove back across the Potomac and gave the key of the box to Mr. Burke. To avoid suspicion, she had left her

10   ANOTHER VERSION OF THIS STORY IS THAT SARAH TRACY AND MARTHA BURKE SEWED THE BONDS IN THEIR PETTICOATS AND BOTH WENT TO WASHINGTON.

eggs on Mr. Riggs' desk, where she had emptied them from
her basket, and with his usual thoughtfulness, he had
tucked the egg money into her little purse.

She drove slowly back along the old road to Mount
Vernon. Soldiers smiled and touched their caps as she went
by. In Alexandria the search for the missing money and
bonds continued. On her return to Mount Vernon she
wrote to Mrs. Comegys, but not one word of her adventure
crept into the letter.

*I must visit Washington again to procure passes. General
McClellan has taken command, and there are new regulations. All
passes must issue from his office or General Scott's. None of the
servants can go to Alexandria, and we have had mail but once in
ten days! I must get proper passes or go myself three times a week
to Alexandria, — or go without mail. This I cannot think of, for I
must keep watch lest anything against Mount Vernon appears.*

*For two miles this side of Alexandria, until I reach Mr. Riggs',
it is nothing but soldiers in the streets and on the boat. Then all the
camps to pass through! For the rest of my life I shall have a dislike
for a gun, or a drum, or a military uniform! Martial music, that
I used to love above all others is nothing but a dirge now, — without
its soothing effect.*

CHAPTER FIVE

THE AUTUMN

OF 1861

About the middle of August there was a skirmish at Pohick Church, six miles below Mount Vernon. Northern pickets had been placed at Hollin Hall, north of Mount Vernon, while in the village of Accotink, just a short distance to the south, Confederate soldiers had arrested the mill owner[11] and taken him to Richmond for questioning. In September, the news was received at the mansion that John A. Washington[12] had been killed near Cheat Mountain in Virginia. He had been on the staff of General Robert E. Lee. At noon on the third of October, the picket guard was recalled from Hollin Hall, and the neighborhood around Mount Vernon quieted down temporarily. On that same

11 PAUL HILLMAN TROTH
12 LAST PRIVATE OWNER OF MOUNT VERNON.

day, a note and a new pass were sent to Miss Tracy from
Colonel Townsend at Army Headquarters in Washington.
Colonel Townsend wrote:

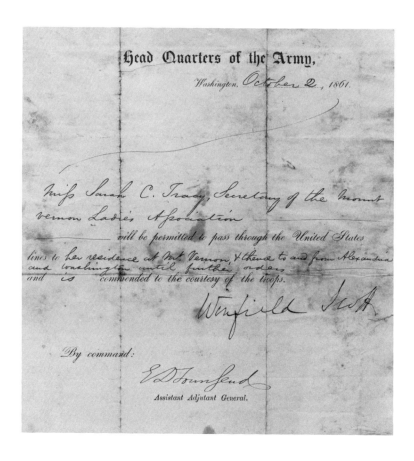

This pass, issued by General Winfield Scott, enabled Sarah Tracy to pass safely through
Union lines on her travels between Mount Vernon, Alexandria, and Washington.
Mount Vernon Ladies' Association.

Dear Miss Tracy,

With your pass, your safeguard for Mount Vernon, and the enclosed order, you have every protection is in the power of General Scott to give. I suppose it is not possible absolutely to prevent annoyances, or even danger, but in such case the immediate commander of the troops would be the proper person to refer to.

Very truly yours,

E. D. Townsend

Headquarters, Washington, October 2, 1861

Miss Sarah C. Tracy, Secretary of the Mount Vernon Ladies Association, will be permitted to pass through the United States lines to her residence at Mount Vernon and thence to and from Alexandria and Washington until further orders and is commanded to the courtesy of the troops.

By command: Winfield Scott

E. D. Townsend

Assistant Adjutant General

Mount Vernon Mansion,

October 9, 1861

My dear Mrs. Comegys,

. . . We are still safe and unmolested, the grand difficulties have been for the present surmounted, but I have "had a time of it"! I believe I wrote you that after issuing the new orders by General McClellan, a month ago, the passes granted the servants were valueless, and I went to Washington to procure them from General

McClellan, himself. He declined *giving them, saying no servants could be trust &c. I came back disappointed, but as I had a pass from General Scott, resigned to be* market woman, *and* mail carrier, *myself, but to my consternation my pass was disputed by the outside pickets, and it was not until I insisted upon seeing the officer, that I could get by. They said they had received orders from General McClellan. I resolved to return to Washington to learn the cause, but the day before I intended to leave, word was brought that Federal pickets had moved down to within three miles of Mount Vernon and had* barricaded the road! *This was a contingency we never thought of, for there seemed no reason for it, but that made no difference, the fact was there, the "outer world" was unapproachable, Finally I became desperate.* Candles and Oil *disappeared entirely, and many small things, considered the necessaries of life, were not to be had. All of this amused me. I laughed until there was* no meat *for the servants! This looked serious, for laborers must be fed, and on something more substantial than would satisfy* me. *I announced my determination to "run the blockade." There were several ways and I intended to try each until I succeeded. I heard of a farmer living some three or four miles west of us whose road had also been blockaded, and who had made himself a way through the woods. From here to his farm the road was open; so I decided to "take to the woods." I started early in the morning not knowing what was before me, but that obstacles must be overcome. Such a ride! My attendant, a negro of admirable sang froid, old enough to be reliable;* my horses, a pair of mules.

With a trembling heart, I confess, I began this wild ride!

We found the woods after many discouraging directions from the farmer. The sky was bright and sunny, and that always gives one courage. We entered the woods and found that where the underbrush was not so thick as to be impassable, the grass was too high to leave any trace of previous waggon tracks. We were constantly being lost. I feared we would be forced into, what my nature revolts against, turning back. For two hours we wandered around, but finally saw a fence, then "the bars," and were ready to shout, for we were "out of the woods"! I went directly to Washington, resolved to find the man, whoever he might be, who could help me. Some said Mr. Cameron, some said Mrs. Lincoln, but with a woman's instinct and faith in those who have proved kind, I went to Headquarters.

General Scott was sick, but my friend Colonel Townsend, a noble, true-hearted man, listened to my story, and requested me to write it all down and send it to him. I did so and received a reply, saying General Scott advised me to see Mr. Lincoln, if his pass was disputed, there was "no power but the President who could help me"! So to Mr. Lincoln I went. He received me very kindly and wrote a note to Mr. McClellan requesting him to see me and arrange the matter in the best way possible. I carried this to General McClellan, who said it was a grand mistake, he had never given an order revoking one of General Scott's passes, he knew his position too well. It was over zeal on the part of the Volunteer officers. He offered to do anything he could for me, would send a steam tug with provisions from time to time, as I might desire, &c. In fact everybody was kind. General Scott gave me a new pass, rather more positive than the first, and also one for Miss McMakin from Philadelphia! She is

now in Washington, I am going up for her tomorrow.

Thus you see we are once more quiet, I have climbed the "Hill Difficulty" once more. I may find myself at the bottom again tomorrow, but I never anticipate. I have found the troubles of today so absorbing as to annihilate those of yesterday, and those of tomorrow too far off to command attention. I have so much to be thankful for. I have found that as the path of duty has been made plain to me; God, who is the strength of the weak and confiding, has gone beside me, smoothing the rough places; and where the help of human friend was needed, placing the kind and willing in my way. The kind approval of yourself and husband, of our good Regent, and the other ladies, is an admirable stimulate.

I have been perfectly well, having had to play doctress not only to nearly everyone here, but also to some still left on Mr. Washington's farm. I, myself, have escaped all ailments.

Poor Mr. Washington's family! Is it not dreadful, six children, in one short year, to lose both father and mother. This is a grief indeed. There need be not the slightest anxiety about Mount Vernon in consequence of his death. When he came here last fall, Miss Cunningham sent for him and everything was arranged, and he

---

When General George B. McClellan would not honor Sarah Tracy's pass from General Winfield Scott, Scott suggested that Miss Tracy appeal directly to President Abraham Lincoln. The president received Miss Tracy at the White House and immediately ordered General McClellan to take care of the matter.

Sarah Tracy Collection Mount Vernon Ladies' Association.

assured her his death would alter nothing. His will was explicit,
and his heirs would never molest Mount Vernon. The title is in Mr.
Riggs' hands.

Mr. Herbert desires his regards. Remember me to all your family.
Many thanks for your kindness.

Yours affectionately,
S. C. Tracy

P.S. I would love to come to see you, but my presence here was
never so necessary. We have a great many soldiers visiting here,
sometimes all day long they are coming, in companies of four or
five, and it requires time of us all. They behave perfectly well now.

A few nights after Miss Tracy wrote this letter, a group of
Confederate Cavalrymen came charging up the road to
Alexandria from the South. They were met at the crossroads
in Accotink by Federal troops. Shots rang out, mingled with
shouts and terse commands. The Quakers in the village left
their beds to seek shelter in the questionable safety of their
cellars. The skirmish lasted until dawn, when each group
withdrew to its own lines. The sounds of firing had been
clearly heard at Mount Vernon, only four miles away, but
not a single soldier had entered the grounds there on any
pretext whatsoever.

And in Washington, General McClellan did not forget his
promise to send supplies to the little group who were caring
for Mount Vernon. A few days after Miss Tracy's visit to
Washington, a small boat carrying provisions docked at the

wharf in front of Mount Vernon. Miss Tracy wrote a letter of appreciation.

> Mount Vernon Mansion
> October 19, 1861

Colonel Hudson, U.S.A.

Dear Sir.

Except if you please the united thanks of our little colony for your successful efforts in sending us our provisions, which arrived in safety on Thursday.

We are much distressed at the unfortunate accident which occurred to the Boat on her return from so kind an errand.

> Very respectfully yours,
> S. C. Tracy

CHAPTER SIX

A YOUNG

LIEUTENANT

In November, red berries shone like rubies on the dogwood trees which grew low in the tall woods around Mount Vernon. Near the mansion large clusters of scarlet berries brightened the dark green holly hedge, and inside the mansion flaming logs glowed in the large fireplaces.

From outside Mount Vernon's gates came the news that the owner of Accotink mills had been released, but he had no sooner returned to his home in the village than he was placed under arrest by another group of Southerners and taken to the prison at Manassas Junction. While this was going on in the neighborhood, soldiers from the Northern Army continued to visit Mount Vernon in complete safety.

One young lieutenant came, intending to stay for a few
hours, and remained for four days. Miss Tracy explained his
visit to Mrs. Comegys.

> *Mount Vernon Mansion*
> *November 30, 1861*

Dear Mrs. Comegys,

*When your letter arrived it found me in a new position, nursing
a sick lieutenant of the 5th Michigan, named Pomeroy. The poor
fellow had been very ill of congestive fever, and was discharged
from the hospital, with the injunction to be prudent. The next day
some of his friends were coming down here and he joined them,
insisting he was fully able. Soon after reaching the house, he was
taken ill, and Mr. Herbert found him under a tree wild with
delirium. He had him brought into the house and he and the
young man's friends did what they could. Miss McMakin and
myself were in town.*

*When we returned we found two or three messengers had been
sent for a doctor, and an ambulance. The poor fellow was on blankets
on the floor in a raging fever, and perfectly unconscious of anything,
and the men frightened lest he would die. Not withstanding which,
they wanted to move him back to camp!*

*I insisted that if forty ambulances came, he should not be
moved, and had him put to bed, mustard foot-bath, mustard
behind his head, and all those other remedies. His Captain and an
ambulance came, but I would not let them move him. He was not
quiet until eleven o'clock, when his friends left him with a Corporal*

to take care of him. His groans were fearful, and his calls upon his wife heartrending. He had been married but one month when he came here.

The next day he had a return of the bad symptoms, but he fought them off. He was with us four days and we sent him back to camp feeling well, without a doctor having seen him.

He was a very agreeable and gentleman-like young fellow and seemed so grateful for what we had done for him. I shall long remember his tone and manner in reply to me when he said it was useless for him to attempt to thank me, for he had no words. I told him we had only done as we would wish others to do for those we loved who were separated from us, and all I asked was that if he found any poor fellow sick or suffering he would think of me, and do what he could for him.

He replied, with full eyes, "So help me God, I will."

I was in Washington on Tuesday to request that an order be given to the Commander of Division, General Heintzelman, forbidding large bodies of troops coming to the place.

After General Scott's order, the soldiers were very particular, and came but few at a time; but since his resignation, they have been less particular. . . . Within a week several hundred have come at once. They trampled over everything.

Long since, Mr. Herbert and I decided there was no way in which we could aid the Association so much as by acting as police, ourselves. He could receive the visitors, show them the house &c; I would take my post in the sitting room, from the windows of which I command a view of the garden walks, General

Pohick Church, only a few miles south of the Mount Vernon estate, was the site of a skirmish
in 1861. Although virtually all valuables were taken from the church, the structure survived.
George Washington had served as a vestryman at Pohick Church from 1762 to 1784.
Mount Vernon Ladies' Association.

*Washington's magnolia, and the holly trees, the leaves of which
are objects of particular interest. In this way we save three or four
dollars a day. When there is a succession of visitors, Mr. Herbert is
in one place. I show the privates the house. I will not the officers,*

they are not polite, excepting those high up. This, of course, takes all our time. . . .

We have some annoyances, but have succeeded in our plan so far. But if they come by hundreds in at the gate, and boat loads at the wharf, fifty policemen could not protect the place. So I posted to the Headquarters Wednesday, and was received with the utmost politeness. Colonel King, on the staff of General McClellan, said "Miss Tracy, General McClellan will do anything you want, only say what you wish." I said what I wished, and he said, "It shall be done."

. . . I have had notices put up requiring an entrance fee of twenty five cents from land visitors. Collected a little, but of course the soldiers plead poverty — many with truth. We are trying to keep these contributions to pay the necessary laborers.

As the year 1861 drew to a close, there were reports of another skirmish down the road at Pohick Church, the sturdy red brick church that had been so dear to the families of General Washington, George Mason, and their well-known friends and neighbors. Everything of value had been stolen from the church, even the heavy white baptismal font was missing. The roof leaked through more than 30 years of neglect, and some of the windows were broken, but the brick walls of the church stood proudly upright.

CHAPTER SEVEN

WAR BETWEEN THE STATES, 1862

In March 1862, a Federal pass, which had been formerly refused a servant at Mount Vernon, was given to Miss Tracy. It read:

March 4, 1862

Let the Bearer, Thomas King, (colored) pass over any Bridge or Ferry to Virginia and return for the purpose of providing marketing for his employer until the thirty-first instant.

March 7, 1862

Captain Moses, Asst. Ajt. General

Dear Sir,

Will you please request of General Heintzelman the repetition, in the various regiments of his Division, of the order issued by Major-General McClellan forbidding soldiers visiting Mount Vernon on Sunday?

So many new regiments have come into the Division since the first issue of the order, that we are quite as much annoyed by their crowding the place on that day as if there had been no such order.

I presume it will not be necessary to request the renewal of the order from "Headquarters," but if this is necessary it can be easily accomplished.

Very respectfully yours,
S. C. Tracy, Sec.,
Mt. V.L.A.

That spring the Mount Vernon boat was permitted to run again from Washington and Alexandria, and the 25–cent entrance fee received from the passengers helped

---

General George B. McClellan, known as "Little Mac," took over command of the Union Armies in November 1861. Like his predecessor Winfield Scott, General McClellan continued to support Sarah Tracy's work at Mount Vernon by granting military passes and sending provisions to the estate.

Sarah Tracy Collection, Mount Vernon Ladies' Association.

defray the expense of keeping the mansion in repair and of paying servant's salaries. Visitors who wished to be admitted to the room in which General Washington died paid an additional quarter for the privilege.

On May 24, 1862, the *Alexandria Gazette* announced: "Mail facilities were yesterday reestablished between Washington, Alexandria and Accotink, Fairfax County, Virginia. . . . The Post Office will be regularly supplied from Alexandria."

From August 27 until September 2, the firing of cannon near Manassas Junction was heard at Mount Vernon. The second battle of Bull Run was another victory for the South, and General Lee's Army, after resting for a day near Chantilly, marched north and crossed into Maryland at Harper's Ferry.

One of the most amusing war stories to be brought to Mr. Herbert at Mount Vernon was about Colonel Mosby's raid on the Federal troops at Fairfax Court House. The Colonel, with 30 picked men, had stolen through the enemy's lines and returned with Brigadier-General Stoughton and 33 Union soldiers as prisoners of war. So successful was this adventure that Colonel Mosby and his rangers continued their raids on the Army of the Potomac, in much the same way that Francis Marion, the "Swamp Fox," harassed the British Army in the Carolinas during the American Revolution.

Following the Federal defeat at Manassas Junction, Secretary of War Stanton stopped the boat from running to

Mount Vernon. Another unhappy result of the battle was that General McClellan was relieved of his command. "Little Mac," as the General was called, had been unusually popular with the soldiers in the Army of the Potomac and was well liked at Mount Vernon.

In December, clouds of dust rose between Mount Vernon and the setting sun. The newly-appointed General Burnside was moving his troops south through the Mount Vernon neighborhood toward Fredericksburg. There he attacked General Lee, who had returned from his march into Maryland. Once again the Confederates were victorious, and the little group at Mount Vernon could hear the rumbling wheels of the horse-drawn cannon as the badly beaten Union Army returned to the North. On December 30, General Burnside was relieved of the command of the Army of the Potomac.

C H A P T E R   E I G H T

W A R   B E T W E E N

T H E   S T A T E S ,

1 8 6 3

January 1863 began with the news that General Joseph Hooker had replaced General Burnside as commander of the Army of the Potomac, that the Mount Vernon boat was to run again, and that speculators were once more planning to build a railroad to Mount Vernon.

Food was becoming a vital problem to the little colony at Mount Vernon, but fortunately there was some food that came within easy reach. From the end of November through January, canvasback ducks flew up the Potomac from Chesapeake Bay. For more than a century this had been the favorite duck in the neighborhood. February and

March were barren months, but about the last week of April shad and herring began to run in the Potomac. Shad was considered a delicacy, as was sturgeon, which was plentiful. The caviar was never served, however. It was either thrown away or buried, for according to the old cooks, "If a chicken eats it, the chicken will surely die."

Herring was referred to by the Friends in the neighborhood as "that rare delicacy and *steady diet*, the herring." Barrels of herring were salted down for the winter, but while the barrels at Mount Vernon were safe in the store house, the Quakers had to keep theirs carefully hidden from both Northern and Southern foraging parties.

In the spring the Union Army suffered one of its worst defeats of the entire war at Chancellorsville, less than 40 miles from Mount Vernon, and word came to the mansion that Stonewall Jackson, the beloved Southern general, had been killed. General Hooker retreated, confused and badly beaten, and was replaced by General Gordon Meade as Commander of the Army of the Potomac. Each time a battle was lost by Federal troops in Virginia and a new commander replaced the old one, Miss Tracy had to make sure that the neutral position of Mount Vernon was clearly understood by him.

All during the summer of '63, through the sweet-smelling Virginia woods, Colonel Mosby's men were riding by night, swiftly and silently down on the Quaker settlement around Mount Vernon. One night a horse would be stolen from the

Woodlawn neighborhood, a mile from Mount Vernon's west gate. On the following night, a stable in the village of Accotink would be emptied. In the morning, Union soldiers would search the neighborhood, without finding a trace of the rangers. If Federal troops remained on guard through the night, the well-informed rangers sat by their own campfires, but as soon as the troops were withdrawn, another raid would be made on the rich little community. One night at Woodlawn Mansion they took the owner, John Mason, and his son William, but set them both free shortly afterwards.

One day, Miss Tracy received word that 82-year-old West Ford, a former servant of Judge Bushrod Washington, was ill, and she sent at once to have him brought to Mount Vernon to be cared for in his old age, one more to feed from the scant supply of food. Ford had come to the mansion with his master in 1802, when Bushrod Washington inherited Mount Vernon from his uncle, George Washington. He had not left Mount Vernon until John A. Washington moved away in 1860, although he had been set free by the terms of his master's will in 1829. He could tell wonderful stories about General and Mrs. Washington, told to him by Billy, one of the General's favorite servants, who was living at Mount Vernon when West Ford first came there.

When summer gave way to fall and the leaves turned brilliant yellow and fiery red, the mallard ducks flew up the river past Mount Vernon, within easy reach of a well-aimed fowling piece. Overhead, in the cold, gray sky, flocks of wild geese flew above the mansion, hesitated, turned, and set off in a new direction.

As winter came, Miss Tracy began to realize the truth of a statement that had appeared in Forney's *Philadelphia Press* in 1858: "Mount Vernon, with nothing to take care of it, would be like the elephant drawn in a raffle – a puzzle to know what to do with it."

CHAPTER NINE

WAR BETWEEN
THE STATES,
1864

Mount Vernon,

January 5, 1864

S o strict are the injunctions of the Government against giving passes, that the few land visitors who came from day to day, leaving a small fee to eke out expenditures, have ceased entirely now; and we have not ten visitors a month! I do not believe there is any remedy until the war is over.

Miss Tracy reviewed her past three years at Mount Vernon in a letter to Mrs. Ritchie, of Virginia.

January 22, 1864

. . . She [Miss Cunningham] wrote me to come down here immediately, feeling sure the presence *of a lady would tend to insure respect toward the place from both contending parties. She hoped to join me soon. She found that impossible, and wrote me to remain, and again urged Mr. Herbert not to abandon his post. I sent for Mary McMakin, and we have been here ever since. All things considered, we have got along very comfortably. We have been a greater part of the time between the Federal and Confederate lines, but no depredations have been committed. Since the first May of the war no Confederates have been on the place. A very large number of Federal soldiers have visited here, but after the first month, in a respectful manner.*

During the second summer of the war, the boat was permitted to run regularly from Washington here, but after the second battle of Bull Run, the Secretary of War would no longer permit passengers to land on the Virginia side. This has been a serious loss to us. No attempt was made to do anything more than keep the place in neat order, and repair the occasional breakage, but even that requires money.

Then unexpectedly, a letter was delivered to Mount Vernon from Miss Cunningham in South Carolina.

This is the third letter I have written to you in reply to yours of January . . . the first tidings received from you for more than two years.[13] *I was dumb with surprise and joy. . . . I was rejoiced to hear*

13   MISS TRACY'S LETTERS TO MISS CUNNINGHAM WRITTEN IN 1862 AND 1863 EVIDENTLY DID NOT REACH THEIR DESTINATION.

Winslow Homer, an artist-correspondent for *Harper's Magazine*, made this
sketch of the Mansion when he stopped at Mount Vernon in 1861 on his way to join the
Army of the Potomac.
Mount Vernon Ladies' Association.

*from you, that all were well and getting on well, and faithful
through all trails to the responsible and precious charge. My faith
in you, and Mary, and Mr. Herbert was so strong that I had
learned to be passive after the first year.*

*Thank you for all of your assurances of faithfulness to me. I felt
from the first that you three were sent as special mercies to me from
my Heavenly Father. Were not my feelings prophetic?*

On February 22, there was a meeting in Washington of the Vice Regents of the Mount Vernon Ladies' Association. Miss Tracy was invited to attend. One matter of vital interest to the three at Mount Vernon was brought up at the meeting. It was decided that Miss Tracy, Miss McMakin, and Mr. Herbert should be paid their salaries, which were long overdue.

As the war continued to cut off Mount Vernon's sources of revenue, Mr. Herbert worked out a plan by which he hoped to raise a little money to defray expenses. His idea was to put aside as many of the bricks that had been made on the Mount Vernon estate as might be needed later for rebuilding and repairing, and then to sell the rest as souvenirs. Miss Tracy wrote to Mrs. Comegys asking permission to try the plan.

Mount Vernon,

March 16, 1864

. . . Mr. Herbert is much obliged for the power to sell the bricks, but he cannot do so now, as he has an elephant to take care of. Mrs. Farnsworth[14] did as she promised, procured permission from Secretary Stanton for General Rucker to sent to Mount Vernon the much desired manure. It came in such quantities that the wharf was more than full, and having but one cart and one wagon, it could be removed but slowly. Mr. Herbert was both exhausted and in despair. I had to write to General Rucker and beg to send no more at present. Everything is to be fertilized.

14 VICE REGENT FOR MICHIGAN.

About 30 miles to the south of Mount Vernon there was a vast woods known as the Wilderness. All during the hot days of May and June, the woods were filled with Confederate and Union soldiers, fighting one of the bloodiest battles of the war. General Grant had begun his relentless drive toward Richmond, capital of the Confederacy.

CHAPTER TEN

WAR BETWEEN THE STATES, 1865

"... Mr. Everett's[15] death, the fall of Fort Fisher, and Butler's disgrace are a singular trio of events to occur at the same time," wrote Miss Tracy from Mount Vernon on January 19, 1865.

January 31, 1865

Dear Mrs. Comegys,

We were nearly two hours going from Alexandria to Washington in the Boat, on account of the ice, and it was such a dangerous performance, ice making constantly as the cold increased, that I

---

15 EDWARD EVERETT WAS THE OUTSTANDING AMERICAN ORATOR WHO CONTRIBUTED THE PROCEEDS OF HIS LECTURES ON GEORGE WASHINGTON TO THE MOUNT VERNON LADIES FOR THE PURCHASE OF MOUNT VERNON, A SUM OF $69,964, MORE THAN ONE-THIRD OF THE PURCHASE PRICE.

decided to return by the cars, and there was but one train. . . . I saw
Mr. Riggs at the bank.

I think we had the coldest ride I ever took, my feet were nearly
frozen when I arrived. I had no sensation in them, could not tell
when they touched the floor. But after having them vigorously
rubbed, I was warm and have had no ill effect. Every day and night
since has been colder than the previous one, but today it has
moderated. I came back with many threats not to see Washington
again until the 22nd. I do dislike cold weather, it unfits me for
everything.

The 22nd of February was the date scheduled for the
yearly meeting of the Vice Regents of the Mount Vernon
Ladies' Association.

March passed, and April, the most beautiful month
along the Potomac, came to Mount Vernon. As darkness fell,
Upton Herbert stood outside the open doorway, on the
long, white-columned piazza of the mansion. Far below, the
river was dark and silent. Across the Potomac, no lights
were visible on the Maryland shore. He turned from the
river as he heard a door to the hall opening. The hallway
was shadowy, almost dark, lighted only by a single candle.
The lantern that had been hung there in 1743 had been
removed in 1802 to Arlington, now in the hands of the
Federal Government, its green lawns a burial place for
Union soldiers. Mary McMakin and Sarah Tracy entered the
hallway and walked over to the small table next to the

stairs. They picked up their own candlesticks and carefully lighted their candles from the one that was burning there. Mary started up the stairs, the bottom edge of her long skirt almost filling the space from the wall to the banister. Miss Tracy waited until she had almost reached the landing. Then taking up her candle in her left hand, and holding the front of her skirt with her right, she followed. The light from her candle fell on her dark hair. Her neck and arms gleamed white. Miss Tracy's waist was small and her skirt voluminous. Her low-heeled slippers were hidden from view as she moved with a steady, effortless motion, up the stairway. Upton Herbert stood watching her from the doorway. Stories of war and heroism kept coming to the mansion, stories of Colonel Mosby's rangers and General Lee's men, of Belle Boyd and her arrest as a Confederate spy. He wondered if Miss Tracy knew how much he longed to be a part of it all; he had said very little to her about it.

He stepped into the hall as Miss Tracy turned at the landing. She paused, her candle held high in her left hand, her right hand resting on the rail, and as though she knew what had been passing in his mind, slowly she smiled down at him. Then bidding him good night, she followed Mary up the stairs. She had known for four long years what a sacrifice he was making to remain at Mount Vernon during the war.

On April 9, 1865, General Lee surrendered his Army to General Grant at Appomattox Court House in Virginia, and a week later came the startling news that President

Abraham Lincoln had been shot and killed.

The summer days passed swiftly. Toward the end of August Miss Tracy wrote:

. . . *The Boat has been running since the first of June. For a month before we had a rush of visitors, every day, and all day long, by land. We have since April made this years expenses! After this all is clear, except what is owing to Mr. Herbert. He left what was due him a year ago to carry on the establishment, up to the first of January last. There is no other debt during the year.*

Mr. Herbert has been preparing the ground for raising such crops as could feed the stock and people necessary here. He has this summer harvested sufficient wheat for the years consumption, or nearly so. He will have an abundance of corn. His crop is the finest around here. He has little rye. Of course he has cabbages, potatoes, etc., in abundance.

During the summer, tired Union soldiers, returning to their homes in the north, paused to visit Mount Vernon, carved their initials in the trees that bordered the lane from West Gate to the mansion and bought bunches of flowers from the gardens. Miss Tracy wrote to Miss Cunningham about the soldiers' desire for flowers.

September 9, 1865

. . . *I had a servant man whom I was paying myself, for he was a necessity to me. I made constant expeditions to town when we*

A sketch from the *New York Illustrated News*, December 16, 1861, depicts soldiers visiting
Mount Vernon. The scene is the park slope between the mansion and the river, with the icehouse
vault entrance and the old summer house in the background.

Mount Vernon Ladies' Association.

had to buy and bring out with us everything used on the place, our drive over bad roads, through camps, pickets, etc., often late at night. A sober, faithful, and reliable man was a necessity. . . . When I did not want him, he worked in the garden. Toward spring I let Mr. Herbert have him all the time in the garden. The two made hot beds and planted the vegetable garden. I was determined I would not live here without flowers. You know I could not live anywhere without. We had some fine roses, some of my own, and some Mr. Herbert had bought for the place. I expended about $8.00, not more, in seeds and planted them for my own comfort. We, Robert, (the servant), Mr. Herbert, and myself, planted, transplanted, and trimmed the plants ourselves. We had just got things in fine condition when came a rush of visits from soldiers. They were crazy for flowers. We had no gardener. Robert had to aid Mr. Herbert with the visitors. He was the only help he had; so Mary and I gathered the flowers, made the bouquets, and sold them. With these flowers we made . . . $300.00.

I had written to Mrs. Comegys for her approval of hiring another man to help in the garden, as at this season there is much work to do, and with it I also want permission for Mr. Herbert to repair some fences.

Of course after October this resource will fail. The first frost will kill the flowers. But then we have another resource. Photographs!

The whole neighborhood, beyond Mount Vernon's fences lay stunned from the effects of the war. Miss Tracy tried to describe its condition, to Miss Cunningham, in the next paragraph of her letter.

I could write volumes of what I know to be the truth, tales that you would scarcely believe. You have had no army twice and thrice through your places — every stalk of grain and hay, and every barn burned. Every hog, sheep, and cow killed. Every pound of wheat and corn taken away, and every horse. Every carriage carried off, and when they could not be, the wheels taken off and burned. . . . I have heard nothing else for three years. But all we see who have lost everything and have to begin life anew, are cheerful, and go to work like men and women! They have tried, and do try, to put aside the past and look only to the future. Alas! it is very hard for some.

While in other parts of the South that fall the Ku Klux Klan and vigilantes were being formed for much-needed protection against the lawless, the Quakers organized the Woodlawn Horse Company,[16] of Fairfax County. The preamble of their constitution stated: "We, the undersigned, citizens of Fairfax County, Va., deem it necessary to our mutual protection against horse-thieves, to form ourselves into a company of which the following is the Constitution." Reading farther along, article six provided that "fifty dollars is ordered as a reward by the company for the capture and conviction of the thief," article nine gave the assurance to members that "any member failing to recover a horse stolen, after due vigilance having been used by the company, he shall be entitled to receive a compensation not to exceed one hundred

16   THE WOODLAWN HORSE COMPANY HELD ITS LAST MEETING AND DISBANDED IN DECEMBER 1944, TURNING OVER THE FUNDS IN ITS TREASURY TO THE ALEXANDRIA HOSPITAL.

dollars. . . ." The company proved so effective that it was not long before the horse and cattle thieves withdrew from the Mount Vernon neighborhood.

As the Confederate soldiers returned to their homes, Miss Tracy wrote:

> . . . Mr. Herbert's brothers are safe and well. Arthur was married in July to a lady from Petersburgh. William is with us now. His cousins are, in the main, alive. He has lost some favorites. . . .

Two weeks later she wrote to Mrs. Comegys about the ancient curse of the Mount Vernon neighborhood, chills and fever.

> . . . Last week we had seven down with chills and fever, and they were a very bad type, taking, unless closely watched, a congestive form, or running into typhoid.
>
> About these photographs. Last winter the Ladies were talking about how good a thing it would be if the Association could have views taken to be sold here. Ever since the war ended we have been excessively annoyed by photographers who wished to take views and give the Association a percentage. This, Miss Cunningham said, she would never consent to, for it was only a way to make money out of Mount Vernon; that the only way was to have someone take the views, paying them so much, the parties not being allowed to sell them, or to give copies, to any but the Association.

Ann Pamela Cunningham, founder and first Regent of the Mount Vernon Ladies' Association.
In the fall of 1860, she had to return to her home in South Carolina and, because of the war,
was unable to come back to Mount Vernon until late 1866.
Mount Vernon Ladies' Association.

I have been since April trying to find someone who would take the views on those terms. Finally a young man was recommended to me by two friends of mine who are scientific men and amateur photographers. They sent out a young man and his brother, the Messrs. Bell. They offered to take the views and give me copies to send the Ladies for approval. My friends lent them their instruments, which were the best money could buy.

*We kept them five days, and they had every chance for fine
lights, etc. I am sure you will admire the pictures as much as others
do. The terms seem very moderate. They have taken cartes de visite,
a size for stereoscope, and what is called cabinet size. . . . Mr. Riggs
says it is very reasonable. Mr. Bell keeps the negatives and supplies
the photographs as demanded, and will never allow them to be
used for anyone but the Association. Please say if this arrangement
meets with your approval, that we may begin to sell as soon as
they are copyrighted. I am sending copies to all of the committee.*

*Mr. Herbert wished me to say that he has exhausted all the
money sent for extra labour, and that he will be obliged to draw
about $40.00 per month more than he has been drawing, in order
to get along. I presume he will have your approval, though he does
not wish to draw it till he hears from you.*

It was then that Miss Cunningham wrote a letter to one
of the Vice Regents, showing how well she understood and
appreciated what Miss Tracy and Mr. Herbert had accomplished during the hard years of the war, and how strongly
she hoped that they might be induced to remain a little
longer at their posts.

*. . . If Miss Tracy would remain at her post this course would
work out well enough, for she is an uncommon woman, and it is,
after all, her administrative ability which carried the Association
through its perils, but . . . I have no hope of inducing her to
continue. . . . She wished to resign in the summer of 1860, but*

agreed to remain. . . . She yielded to my entreaties to give the protection of woman to the place; for I was afraid that some pleas would be resorted to as a pretext to seize it. . . . I did not dream that by this she would encounter a life of severe trial and impaired health for five years' duration . . . .

She urges my going as soon as I can; she and Mr. Herbert do not wish to give the place into any hands but mine. Mr. Herbert, whom I thought a fixture for life, intends to resign, as he has been an annual martyr to chills and fever.

A lady came South in December, 1864, under a flag of truce. Had a conference with Miss Tracy before coming; said they had been nearly starved out of Mount Vernon, but that they would hold on! . . . She tells me that the Vice-Regents could attempt no method of raising funds to relieve their troubles . . . as I was regarded as a rabid Secessionist. . . . If things are left to go on for another season — there has been three thousand dollars taken in from May until September, enough to carry them through — I am not in fact needed . . . .

Of her own work, Miss Tracy wrote in December, "I do assure you, keeping all accounts *and* keeping house is rather an exciting and absorbing occupation."

Mary McMakin went home for Christmas that year, and Miss Tracy sent for Mr. Herbert's sister to spend Christmas with them in the Mount Vernon mansion, and to remain with her while Mary was away.

"For the sake of propriety," said Miss Tracy.

CHAPTER ELEVEN

WITHOUT THE
ARMIE'S PROTECTION,
1866

The war had been over for a year, and still no one had come to Mount Vernon to relieve Miss Tracy of her responsibilities. The city of Washington was filled with visitors, and interest in Mount Vernon had quickened. The boat was making two trips a week, bringing sightseers to the mansion. The boat trip was safe and beautiful; the mansion and grounds quiet and peaceful. If the Northern sightseers had returned to Washington by land, however, the trip might have been a revelation to them, for the road up from Mount Vernon to Alexandria was infested with highwaymen. No woman could ride alone beyond her own immediate neighborhood, at any time of day, and no man traveling alone was safe on the road after sundown. As Miss Tracy expressed it:

It has been dangerous to ride in lonely places and even in Alexandria it was not at one time safe to go out alone in the evening. I have had more fear in returning home lately, than during the entire war, and during the past winter have always hastened home earlier than ever before. It was so easy to rob and murder!

On April 11, 1866, Miss Tracy wrote about the Mount Vernon boat:

After next week the trips will be tri-weekly. Of course we personally dread it. Every day will be "Boat Day" or "The Day Before"!

April 26, 1866
. . . I have a sewing machine on which I can do a heap of work. Seamstresses are as scarce as gold, and dressmakers unheard of as far as we are concerned. I consider that when the ladies requested me to take charge and remain in charge, the duties included every-thing necessary to the proper care of the place; as much mending, as accounts, marketing, sweeping, and dusting, when everyone else was ill. The duties are comically diversified.

One of the duties that was somewhat out of the ordinary was that of catching fish for breakfast. Each evening, Mr. Herbert, Miss Tracy, and Mary McMakin went fishing down on the wharf, for as George Washington himself had written, many years before, the Potomac was "a river well stocked with various kinds of fish at all seasons of the year, and in the spring with shad, bass, sturgeon, etc., in abundance."

One evening, just as the tide was coming in swift and strong, the two girls went down alone to do their fishing. Mr. Herbert was busy on another part of the estate. Suddenly, without warning, Mary stepped too close to the edge of the wharf and fell into the deep water. Miss Tracy turned to see her being carried away. Mary fought hard against the tide. She tried to swim toward the wharf, but her wet skirts hampered her.

Miss Tracy took one look up the path to see if help was near and saw that there were no men about. Quickly un-fastening her full skirt at the waist, she pulled it off over her head. Holding one edge of the hem, she cast it out toward Mary. The skirt opened up like a giant parasol and rested gently on the water. Mary caught hold of it, and in another minute or two, Miss Tracy had pulled her back to safety.

When Miss Cunningham suggested that perhaps they should have more help at Mount Vernon, Miss Tracy wrote in reply:

Mount Vernon,

May 18, 1866

. . . *As for hiring anyone to assist us, it is no easy matter. We would, any of us, rather do double duty then take, for the sake of assistance, anyone into our circle who is not perfectly congenial to all. It is very difficult to find persons whom we can trust.*

I tried, for a long time, to get a boy to sell photographs; was finally obliged to take one of old West's grandsons who can count money. As soon as Mr. Herbert can get a trustworthy man, I am going to teach my Robert to make bouquets. He has taste and can learn, but it has been hard to get faithful assistance; so that, except when it is necessary to have him drive me to town, I have given him up to Mr. Herbert.

We have a good gardener, but he cannot make a Bouquet that will sell; so we have to do it. And old Jim sells them, but he cannot count; so he stands under the window and one of us makes change through the blinds!

. . . *Mine is not the easiest task in the world, to make both ends meet. To contrive that peas, beans, cabbage, and flowers shall pay for rakes and hoes; flowers and photographs shall pay a gardener; that bricks shall pay for little odds and ends of plastering, brick-laying, etc., and then when these fall short, and the corn has failed, or been stolen from the fields as it was last year, and feed is to be bought, to contrive where we can pinch out the means to foot the bill. Mr. Herbert is very good at managing these things.*

The photographs of Mount Vernon proved to be very popular with visitors, as Miss Tracy explained in a letter.

. . . The photographs of different sizes are sold, Cartes de visite 25 cents, stereoscopic views — 50 cents, cabinets — 75 cents. I think we will make about $600.00 a year by them.

Early in August, Miss Tracy wrote to Miss Cunningham:

I hope you will come as soon as possible, and that you will call a Grand Council, not an annual meeting. . . . I shall be glad when I can give some definite answer to the incessant inquiries "When is Miss Cunningham coming back" and "When is there to be a meeting?"

Shortly after writing this letter, Miss Tracy, who had been nurse and doctor to the estate for five long years, became ill. All her lovely laughing courage left her, and she begged that someone come to relieve her of the care and responsibility of Mount Vernon so that she might move away from the chills and fever that rose dragon–like from the swamps west of the mansion, and each summer claimed new victims.

At a meeting of the Council of the Mount Vernon Ladies' Association in November, Miss Cunningham was present for the first time in six years, but no plans were made to replace Miss Tracy at Mount Vernon. The minutes of the meeting stated: "A resolution was also passed expressing their [the Mount Vernon Ladies] unqualified approval of the manner in which the Superintendent and the Secretary had discharged the arduous duties committed to their charge. They are grateful to find that with limited means, and under difficult circumstances, the Mansion and grounds under their charge have been so well preserved and protected."

A picture of the ladies at the Council is suggested in a note written by Miss Tracy just prior to the meeting:

. . . I have but a moment to say — do not shorten your dresses that are intended for house or dress, at least not in the back. Small hoops, but long trains are worn.

CHAPTER TWELVE

PEACE ON THE

POTOMAC

Another spring came to Mount Vernon. The dogwood and the judas trees were in full bloom. The countryside began to stir, and fields were being plowed for the wheat and corn that would be harvested in peace. On the river, white sails carried long, low boats past Mount Vernon's wharf, and on the roads, mail was being delivered to the north and to the south. In July a letter was delivered to Miss Tracy at Mount Vernon.

Depot Quartermaster's Office,

Washington, D.C., July 5, 1867

Miss Tracy,

Mount Vernon, Virginia,

Madam,

I have the honor to enclose herewith for your signature duplicate blank receipts for the ambulance sold and delivered to you a few days since, which please sign and return to me.

Please send me the money for the ambulance, to wit $34.00 for which my receipt is also herewith.

Respectfully,

Your obedient servant,

Charles H. Tompkin.

Miss Tracy had bought the ambulance so that invalids and people unable to bear the fatigue of climbing the hill from the wharf to the mansion might ride in comfort. She wrote Miss Cunningham:

. . . Have paid expenses and have a little over this month. Not as many visitors as the last two years. Everyone seems to have gone to Europe.

In another letter she suggested, half in earnest,

. . . I think you had better go and appoint a meeting in Paris in October. You will have a larger attendance there than in this country.

The summer before, Miss Tracy had made bracelets of coffee beans that she sold to visitors to Mount Vernon. This year, however, she found that the man who had bored the holes in the beans was too busy to do the job again. She tried to buy a drill to do the work herself. When this plan also failed, she turned all of her attention to her flowers.

. . . I have made with my own hands over 800 bouquets, which has paid for the superphosphates, farm tools, etc., and we have nearly enough to put a new zinc roof on the Tomb, which is an absolute necessity, the mending we did last fall not being sufficient. The plants and flower seeds I bought with my own money.

In December, the Regent met with the Vice Regents at Mount Vernon. The banquet hall was still bare and unfur-nished, so they used the west parlor, the room usually referred to by Miss Tracy as the sitting room. A report of the meeting states briefly: "A meeting of the Grand Council of the Regent and Vice-Regents of the Mount Vernon Ladies' Association was held at Mount Vernon, the second of December, 1867. . . . Without transacting any business, the meeting adjourned to re-assemble in Washington City the next day. . . . Miss S. C. Tracy then resigned her situation as Secretary of the Association. Miss Tracy was requested to retain her situation till the first of January, and to remain at Mount Vernon as long after as suited her convenience."

Miss Cunningham told the meeting that she intended to move into the Mount Vernon mansion and make it her headquarters. Mary McMakin was remaining as her secretary, and Mr. Herbert had consented to continue as Super-intendent for one more year. The contract with the boat company was left with Mr. Herbert to arrange.

The only known photograph of Upton Herbert, far right, who served as the
first resident superintendent of Mount Vernon from 1859 to 1869. The woman third from
left in the photograph is identified as Sarah Tracy.
Mount Vernon Ladies' Association.

The next four weeks passed swiftly at Mount Vernon. Christmas came and went, and the New Year, 1868, arrived. Then before those in the mansion or out in the quarters had quite realized what was happening – beyond the walks to the flower gardens, beyond Mount Vernon's gate with its crumbling lodges – Miss Tracy had gone!

That might have been the end of the story, except for a final letter in the archives at Mount Vernon, a letter that opens a new chapter in the story of Sarah Tracy and Upton Herbert and casts a different and rather lovely light on all of the preceding chapters.

In 1886, the Mount Vernon Ladies, realizing the drama that had been enacted at Mount Vernon during the War Between the States, wrote to Sarah Tracy and asked if she would send them whatever memoranda she had kept of the period. She replied:

Muckruss

March 25, 1886

My dear Mrs. Comegys,

Your kind letter of the 19th was forwarded to me here, and on my return from a few days in Washington, I found it awaiting me.

Our house burned the Friday before Christmas. Since then, we have made our headquarters here, at Colonel Arthur Herbert's, about three miles from Alexandria. We are making arrangements to build again, but no other house can ever be to us, what that pile of ashes was!

The house was old, and when the air reached the flames, it burst rapidly. We saved most of our silver, private papers, and clothing. The furniture of the parlor and our bedroom on the same floor was saved. Nothing from the second floor, dining room, or kitchen, or store room! It has been a severe blow to us — this utter obliteration of so much that was precious. The pecuniary loss is great, but there was, of course, much that money could not buy and cannot replace. . . .

In one small trunk was packed some family letters from my grandfather and others from Miss Cunningham, and all the memoranda from Mount Vernon. It was burned.

The Herbert family records and the records of the family of the Hon. William Fairfax of Belvoir show that in 1872, Upton Herbert and Sarah C. Tracy were married in Philadelphia. For 14 years they made their home at Bleak House, Upton Herbert's Virginia estate, which was located about five miles from Fairfax Court House. When their house burned in 1885, they built another, in which they lived the rest of their lives. When they died, they were buried in Ivy Cemetery, Fairfax County, Virginia. They had no children.

Years before, Miss Cunningham, first Regent of the Mount Vernon Ladies' Association of the Union, left a tribute to Sarah Tracy among the records, as she wrote: "My secretary and friend," then added, "for *she is a lovely woman.*"

Index